# CONTENTS

# Notes on the Contributors


| | |
|---|---|
| Pablo Bifani | Professor of Economics, Universidad Autónoma, Madrid, Spain |
| Edwin Clark II | Secretary, Department of Natural Resources and Environmental Control, State of Delaware, Dover, Delaware, USA |
| Tom Jones | Administrator, Environment Directorate, Organization for Economic Co-operation and Development, Paris, France |
| Laurent Mermet | Environmental Consultant, ASCA Consultants, Paris, France |
| Kerry Turner | Senior Lecturer in Environmental Economics, University of East Anglia, Norwich, UK |
| Carlos Montes | Professor of Ecology, Universidad Autónoma, Madrid, Spain |

# WETLANDS: MARKET AND INTERVENTION FAILURES

Edited by Kerry Turner
and
Tom Jones



EARTHSCAN PUBLICATIONS LIMITED
LONDON

First published 1991 by
Earthscan Publications Ltd
3 Endsleigh Street, London WC1H 0DD



British Library Cataloguing in Publication Data
Wetlands: Market and intervention failures.
I. Turner, Kerry II. Jones, Tom
333.91

ISBN 1-85383-102-6

Production by Bob Towell
Typeset by Bookman Ltd, Bristol
Printed and bound by Guernsey Press Ltd

Earthscan Publications Ltd is an editorially independent subsidiary
of the International Institute for Environment and Development
(charity number 800066)

# ACKNOWLEDGEMENTS

The authors are indebted to the participants in a November 1989 OECD Workshop on Market and Intervention Failures in Wetland Management. In particular, the contributions of Claude Henri (Ecole Polytechnique, Paris), Ed Maltby (University of Exeter, UK), and Pat Dugan (International Union for the Conservation of Nature, Geneva) are gratefully acknowledged.

Special thanks are also due to Susan Derbez, for her tireless efforts in typing and retyping the manuscript.

# PREFACE

Increased voter-concern for the environment has forced governments to seek more efficient approaches to environmental problems. Wider use of market mechanisms may provide some help in this regard. However, markets often fail properly to value and allocate scarce environmental resources. Another area where efficiency improvements may be available is in the design and delivery of government programmes affecting the environment. However, once again, the full potential of this option is often not realized, due to poor co-ordination and implementation of these policies.

Overcoming both of these types of failure – market and policy intervention – represents an opportunity for achieving environmental improvements and economic improvements at the same time. In short, the elimination of market and intervention failures in the environment would be a solid step in the direction of what the Brundtland Commission has called "sustainable development". This has been a focus of recent work within the Environment Directorate of the Organization for Economic Co-operation and Development (OECD).

Significant evidence exists that wetlands in many countries have been, and remain, subject to stress from a variety of market- and government-policy forces. This fact prompted OECD to commission case studies on how market and intervention failures are affecting wetland management in four countries: the United States of America, the United Kingdom, France, and Spain. This book presents the results of these four case studies. An introductory chapter has also been added, discussing the principles of sustainable development in a wetland management context.

Each chapter represents the opinions of its author(s), and does not necessarily reflect the views of the OECD.

# 1

# SUSTAINABLE WETLANDS: AN ECONOMIC PERSPECTIVE

Kerry Turner

## Introduction

The analysis and case study examples in this book have been brought together to address five important questions concerning wetland ecosystems:

1 What is the current status of the world's wetlands (with special focus on OECD countries)?
2 If wetland losses are significant, why should society be concerned? Are wetlands valuable, and can their worth be quantified in monetary terms?
3 Is it the case that valuable wetland resources are not being managed properly (that is, optimally, in economic terms), resulting in socially inefficient resource use?
4 If this social inefficiency exists, what is the source of the problem?
5 What can/should be done about the problem?

Most of the book focuses on temperate wetlands, although the general principles discussed are also applicable to tropical wetlands in developing countries. Nevertheless, there is a general lack of available information in the literature concerning tropical wetlands and their valuation (Barbier, 1989; Turner, 1990).

The case studies presented in the book demonstrate that wetlands are very valuable, multifunctional environmental resources. Despite this fact, they have been disappearing at an alarming rate all over the globe. All wetlands are under threat from a variety of local or regional human activities. Now the perilous state of coastal wetlands is being even further threatened by one of the consequences of global warming. If the "greenhouse effect" actually operates as predicted, mean sea levels may rise as much as one metre by the year 2100 (Thomas, 1986).

Such an accelerated increase in average sea levels would have serious impacts on the worldwide distribution of coastal wetlands. Salt, brackish and freshwater marshes in temperate zones, and mangroves and other swamps in tropical zones would be inundated or eroded (Turner, Kelly and Kay, 1990). Some wetlands would be able to migrate inland, but others would be prevented from doing so by coastal engineering structures. Although many wetlands have kept pace naturally with historic sea level rises, due to sediment entrapment and peat formation, the vertical accretion of wetlands has never been observed to occur at rates comparable to those projected for sea level rise in the next century.

The threat of global warming simply reinforces the fact that policy-makers need to formulate and implement a much more *sustainable management approach* to wetland stocks. Wetlands are, of course, not the only environmental resources that require "better" management, and the recent "sustainability" debate has been concerned with the development of entire economic systems and their ecological foundations. A few words about this debate are in order to set the stage for what follows (Pearce and Turner, 1990; Turner, 1988a; Pezzey, 1989; and Pearce, Markandya and Barbier, 1989).

## Sustainable economic development

During the past decade, the focus of the environmental debate has shifted from the need for absolute limits on growth toward the need for more sophisticated, relative limits.

Figure 1.1 illustrates the basic model of sustainable economic development (SED) that has emerged since the publication of the influential report by the Brundtland Commission, *Our Common Future* (WCED, 1987).

The Brundtland Commission defined sustainable development as "development that meets the needs of the present

## Figure 1.1: Principles and practice of sustainable development in the wetlands context

**Global ongoing loss of temperate and tropical wetlands**

*Sustainability principles*

Efficiency and equity within and between generations; efficiency and equity objectives are secured by actual compensation; rejection of potential welfare concept.

↓

Much environmental degradation is due to a combination of information, market and intervention failures.

↓

Actual compensation is operationalized via three types of capital transfer in order to pass on a portfolio of productive opportunities of equal or greater value to the next generation:

"CRITICAL" NATURAL CAPITAL + OTHER NATURAL CAPITAL + MAN MADE CAPITAL

$K_NC$ ‹ VERY LIMITED SUBSTITION ‹ $K_N$ ‹ GREATER SUBSTITION › $K_M$

$K_NC + K_N + K_M$ = TOTAL CAPITAL STOCK

Valuation of the capital stock: total economic value = use + option + existence values.

↓

Management of the multifunctional natural capital stock to ensure sustainable flow of income and conservation of the total resource stock.

↓

Extended cost-benefit analysis can provide a sound methodological base for sustainable resource management.

*Practice*

Balance to be struck between wetland conservation, sustainable utilization and economic development; *sustainable utilization* the key concept for wetlands in those countries in which wetlands have already been heavily transformed by human intervention.

Conservation is the priority for countries which still retain extensive areas of relatively unmodified wetlands; and conservation of high value wetlands is a priority in all countries. NO NET-LOSS PRINCIPLE the basic policy objective.

↓

Wetlands loss rate is high and has been caused by "natural" resource-use conflict together with information, market and intervention failures, that is, lack of awareness and appreciation of the full value of the wetlands; pollution damage and overutilization because of open access; and inefficient or inconsistent policy.

↓

Wetlands to be differentiated in terms of their structural and functional value; not all wetlands are equally valuable, but most are mutifunctional assests with extensive environmental capacities/infrastructures; wetlands inventory (regional, national and international) required; identification of actual and potential threats to wetlands, because they are open systems, off-site water – basin-wide analysis is required. No net-loss objective a relative not an absolute constraint, substition possibilites.

↓

Total economic value of wetlands stock is very high; monetary valuation methods and techniques available for some but not yet all of the wetland functions and services.

↓

Ongoing and anticipatory assessment process; standard project appraisal methods augmented by shadow project analysis – wetland creation, transfer and restoration possibilities and costs; integrated water-basin management is the longer-term objective, which will require CBA plus other non-monetary assessment methods.

*Source:* Adapted from Turner (1991).

without compromising the ability of future generations to meet their own needs". Economists are familiar with this as the Pareto criterion for establishing an increase in the overall welfare of society. In practical cost-benefit analysis (CBA), the Pareto criterion is modified, in order to reduce its restrictiveness, to incorporate the idea of "potential compensation". Thus, there is an increase in potential welfare if those who gain from a policy or project could, hypothetically, compensate those who lose. Although the idea of *potential* welfare is consistent with the criterion of economic *efficiency*, it is not consistent with the criterion of *equity*. An equity-orientated approach would require that gainers must *actually* compensate losers.

Most definitions of sustainable development accept the equity principle, in the sense that they require a non-declining (and unimpaired) stock of capital assets (in value terms) to be transferred from one generation to the next. According to this analysis, the aggregate stock is made up of three components: "critical" natural capital ($K_NC$), "other" natural capital ($K_N$) and man-made capital ($K_M$). The $K_NC$ category is composed of vitally important ecosystems and processes, which by definition are of very high value.

If future generations are not to be made worse off by present-day activities, they require the same potential economic opportunities for improving their welfare as the current generation enjoys. The portfolio of capital assets must therefore be managed in such a way as to preserve this potential. The three elements of total capital stock should be viewed as part of a continuum, with each element being more or less substitutable for the other. Exactly which natural capital is considered critical for present and future generations, and the extent to which different types of natural and man-made capital may substitute for each other in years to come, is somewhat uncertain. But there is a strong policy message in this uncertainty, which says that when dealing with potentially essential resources that may be irreplaceable, decision-makers should adopt risk-averse strategies and favour conservation over development.

This model of sustainable development requires that the three types of capital stock eventually be reduced to a common index for comparative purposes. A monetary unit is the yardstick that is usually selected for this purpose. Therefore, the question of valuation becomes very important. As we will see later, the valuation problem is particularly difficult in the case of "critical" natural capital.

Once the different types of capital have been valued, the scene is set for management action to maximize efficiency in the use of that capital, and to fulfill the intergenerational equity objective. Extended cost-benefit analysis can provide an appropriate framework in which these management decisions can be taken.

## Wetlands and sustainable development

We now examine the position of wetlands in this sustainable economic development model. The "Practice" column of figure 1.1 illustrates the state of the wetland situation under each of the critical natural capital, other natural capital and man-made capital headings discussed above. A few generalizations will clarify figure 1.1 and set the scene for the more detailed discussion in succeeding chapters. In the case of temperate wetlands in developed countries, where wetland stocks have already been heavily transformed by human intervention, *sustainable utilization* should be the key management concept.

Sustainable utilization should also be the main priority in managing tropical wetlands in developing countries. The control of population growth, as well as the expansion of economic opportunities available to the current generation (given their relative poverty) are essential elements of such a strategy. As has already occurred in developed countries, wetlands stocks in developing nations should be routinely tapped to increase the flows of income from these assets. However, unlike in developed countries, care should be taken to avoid overexploiting these resources in the development process. In other words, maximum *sustainable* income flows should be the objective.

On the other hand, conservation (that is, management of the rate of change in ecosystems) should be the priority for those developed countries which still retain extensive areas of relatively unmodified wetlands. Conservation of "high-value" temperate wetlands should also be a priority in all countries, both developed and undeveloped. Conservation of "high-value" wetlands is typically an international – not just a national – priority, and may require international compensatory mechanisms when applied to developing nations, for example debt for nature swaps.

As noted earlier, practical experience indicates that wetland losses are continuing at alarming rates in many parts of the world. The reasons for these losses typically involve a combination of market- and policy-intervention failures. A review of these failures in some countries comprises the major focus of this book.

Whichever management strategy is chosen, it will not be costless, so it is very important that wetlands be correctly valued. Overall, the most appropriate type of management system (including the option of converting wetlands with or without compensation) will depend on such factors as: biological conservation needs; the wetland functions and services requiring protection, and their total economic value; regional economic opportunities; adjacent land-use patterns; as well as some factors specifically relevant to developing economies, such as the subsistence needs of local people, and the availability of environmentally-sensitive aid flows (Turner, 1989).

We now return to the five questions posed earlier and begin with a summary of available information about wetland losses.

## Wetland losses

Wetland ecosystems account for about six per cent of the global land area and are considered by many authorities to be among the most threatened of all environmental resources. During the twentieth century, wetland loss rates have generally been very high. Both the physical extent of wetlands and their quality (in terms of species diversity, etc.) have declined. Most of the physical losses have been due to the conversion of wetlands to other land uses, for example industrial, agricultural and residential. But qualitative degradations – for example chemical and biological – have also occurred, with more subtle, complex and longer-term results. The risks of degradation have been increased by the "open-system" nature of wetland resources. This has made wetlands especially prone to damage caused by activities located a considerable distance away from the wetland site, but still within the drainage basin.

Although areas such as North America and Australia retain significant and relatively pristine wetland stocks, these stocks are nothing like as large as they once were. In most of Europe, the amount of wetlands acreage that remains is only a fraction of the original stock, and is often close to, or below, critical threshold levels. Precise loss estimates on a national basis are not generally available. Several OECD countries did implement policy changes, beginning in the mid-1970s, designed to slow down wetland conversion but the impact of these policy changes has not been sufficiently monitored for a clear judgement to be made about their success. Nevertheless, there is a strong probability that wetland losses continue to be high in many OECD economies.

On a global scale, the extensive tropical wetland resources in developing economies are also undergoing changes, due to improved access to wetland zones; to the pressures of population growth; and to economic development generally. Extensive areas of tropical wetland are being lost, either as a direct result of conversion to intensive agriculture, aquaculture or industrial use, or through more gradual qualitative changes caused by hydrological perturbation, pollution and unsustainable levels of grazing and fishing activities.

Goodland and Ledec (1989) have remarked that, until two or three decades ago, a large proportion of the world's wildlands (including wetlands) were protected by their remoteness, their vastness and their marginal usefulness for agriculture, or other economic activities. The last thirty years or so, however, have witnessed the rapid conversions of wetlands in all developing countries.

Mangrove swamps, for example, are rapidly disappearing throughout Asia and Africa, because of land reclamation, fishpond construction, mining and waste disposal. In the Philippines alone, some 300 000 ha (67 per cent) of the national mangrove stock has been lost over the period 1920–80. Other wetland types have suffered equally rapid losses. In Nigeria, the flood plains of the Hadejia River have been significantly reduced as a result of dam construction. Qualitative degradation is also a serious problem – the majority of coastal wetlands in Brazil have been degraded by pollution.

Each of the case studies examined in this book – USA, UK, France and Spain – contain considerable evidence to support the presumption that wetland losses are also occurring in developed nations.

The next important question to pose is, why should we be concerned about the loss of wetlands? To answer this question, we need to know something about the total economic value of these ecosystems. It is the value of this stock, and of the income streams from it, which will be lost if wetlands continue to be destroyed. As such, "value" becomes a yardstick for measuring wetlands policy failures or successes. Unfortunately,the process of valuing the social utility of wetlands is very difficult.

## The economic importance of wetlands

Given the "open-system" nature of wetlands, at least a catchment-wide evaluation of wetland services is required if the full range of these services is to be properly computed. In the past, the geographic extent of wetland benefits was not well-appreciated, but there is now a growing awareness that most wetlands are valuable economic resources, even when retained in their natural or semi-natural state. The conversion or degradation of these natural capital assets will, therefore, often not represent a net increase in social welfare.

Social inefficiency in wetland use is connected to the fact that wetlands are typically under heavy pressure, involving multiple-use conflicts. The inefficiency results not from the conflict itself, but from the fact that not all uses are properly accounted for. This is especially true of the "natural" services provided by wetlands, for example ground water storage, food web support and so on, but is often also true of services provided directly by wetlands to humans – recreation, hunting and so on.

All of the case studies below provide specific examples of the types of economic services provided by wetlands. To help structure this discussion, it is useful to think in terms of the concept of "total economic value" as embodying several types of social benefit.

First, the wetland ecosystem structure – that is the tangible items, such as plants, animals, fish, soil and water – yields benefits which are of *direct use value* to humans. Many tropical wetlands are being directly exploited to support human livelihoods. A large number of fish species depend upon wet-lands in one way or another, and fish represents around twenty cent of the animal protein intake of Africans. In contrast, e level of direct exploitation of this type is small for most emperature wetlands, with the possible exception of fishing and reed harvesting in some locations. Temperate wetlands tend to be more important for other reasons.

Second, the interaction between wetland hydrology and topology, saturated soil and emergent vegetation generally determines the characteristics and the significance of the processes that occur in a wetland. These processes are subsequently responsible for the functional services which provide *indirect use values* – that is the indirect support and protection provided to people, economic activity and property. Storm buffering and pollution retention are two examples of this type of service.

Wetlands also yield *non-use values* (existence value). These are values that are not derived from direct or indirect uses of the wetland. Thus, wetland habitats, and the flora and fauna that these habitats support, may be valued even by humans living far away from the wetland. Even if these people never actually visit the wetland, they may nevertheless feel a sense of loss if such "wild" places ceased to exist. This loss would reduce their option, or that of their descendants, to visit such sites (option value). It would also reduce their ability to pass on undegraded wetlands to future generations (bequest value).

"Option-value" losses can also be interpreted as a loss of the opportunity to gain information about the real value of wetlands as time passes: if the resource is destroyed, the opportunity to gain information about it is destroyed with it. Similarly, existence value may be more broadly defined in order to encompass the notion of "valuing" wetlands on behalf of other (non-human) species (Pearce and Turner, 1990).

The contributory benefits of wetlands extend beyond the boundaries of the wetland itself, and for some classes of wetland, may be globally significant. Wetlands support migratory fish and bird populations of international importance. It was this latter aspect of wetland value that led to the establishment of the Ramsar Convention.

Many scientific uncertainties still surround the precise extent and significance of wetland functions and services, so it is not possible to calculate the marginal economic product of a given wetland accurately. There is also considerable uncertainty about the potential aggregate role that remaining global wetland stocks play in the biosphere, say, for example, as greenhouse gas sinks. Enough evidence is available, however, to demonstrate that wetlands are important ecosystems which will often yield significant structural and functional benefits.

Therefore, the world's wetlands infrastructure embodies significant *total economic value* (defined much more broadly than just "direct use" value). In fact, "total economic" value is made up of actual use value (direct and indirect) plus option value (including bequest value) plus existence value. This approach to valuation is based on the traditional explanation of how value occurs. That is, it is based on the interaction between a human subject (the valuer) and objects (things to be valued). Individuals hold their own values, which result in the objects they observe being assigned different values.

## Valuing wetland services

The four case studies following point out that only wetland use values and other commercial outputs – for example recreation, flood protection, storm-buffer functions – are readily measurable in monetary terms. Nevertheless, available environmental economics literature indicates that non-use values (option and existence values) may be significant, in terms of people's willingness to pay, for a wide range of environmental resources, such as wetlands.

Some progress has been made by economists in attempting to determine empirical (monetary) measures of both environmental use value and non-use values. None of the techniques – indirect methods, travel cost, hedonic pricing and contingent valuation – that have been utilized are problem-free, but enough empirical work has been undertaken to indicate that humans do value the environment positively. Interestingly, non-use values appear to be significantly positive. On the other hand, studies attempting to value tropical wetlands are far less numerous, and are typically restricted to direct use valuations (Barbier, 1989; Dixon, 1989; Turner, 1990).

The social benefit of wetland conservation is the total

economic value (TEV) of the asset that is conserved. The social cost is the forgone value of (non-conservation) uses. The change in the TEV as the amount of the conserved asset is varied is its "shadow price". If the shadow price deviates from the market price, it would be socially beneficial to "correct" the market price. This correction is often made through the use of market instruments such as taxes, subsidies, fines and so on.

Given the wide range of services provided by wetlands, and the difficulty of expressing the value of some of these services in monetary terms, it seems reasonable to assume that the actual value of wetlands in OECD countries is much higher than has usually been assumed. In turn, it is also likely that these wetlands have not been managed in an economically efficient way, generally because resource users have lacked economic signals which reflect the full social costs and benefits of their use. Overutilization, often leading to complete destruction of the wetland, is inevitable in these circumstances. As we will see later, sustainable management of wetlands will often require the use of economic instruments that change market incentives.

The precise factors accounting for the overuse of wetlands are examined later. But there seems little doubt that any radical alteration of remaining wetlands stocks will result in significant net losses in social value. But counteracting these losses will inevitably require policy-makers to have a sense of how big the various wetlands values actually are. Although this book is not the place to review in detail the range of methodologies that have emerged to assist in this valuation process, figure 1.2 and table 1.1 illustrate the different components of the total economic value of wetlands; the techniques available, in principle, to quantify the monetary measure of these benefits; and the most relevant empirical studies that have been undertaken to date.

All of the empirical studies identified in table 1.1 attempt to measure the value of wetlands in one way or another. Depending on the method used, and the particular assumptions that are made, empirical studies can yield quite varying results. Despite this variability, the important message from these studies is that the non-use benefits of wetlands are usually very significant, no matter how they are measured. It is simply

**Figure 1.2: Wetland benefits valuation**

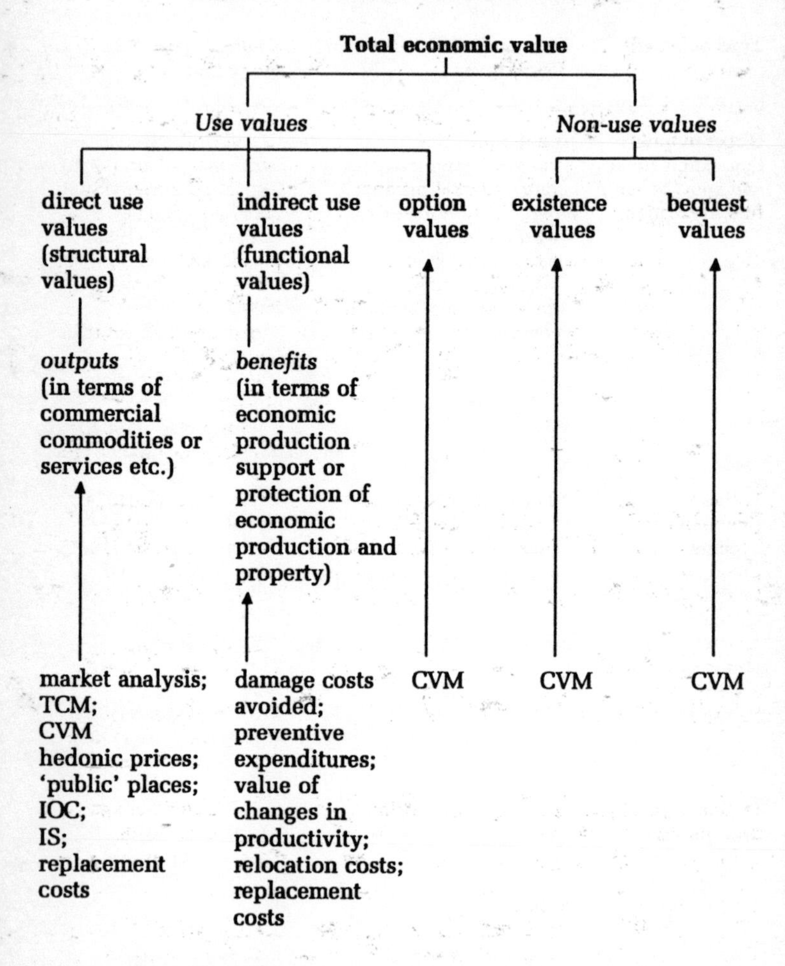


Notes: CVM = contingent valuation method
TCM = travel cost method
IOC = indirect opportunity cost approach
IS = indirect substitute approach

*Source:* Adapted from Barbier (1989)

**Table 1.1: Valuation of wetland structure and functions**

| Type of benefit | Economic valuation Techniques | Studies reported in the literature |
|---|---|---|
| **Direct outputs** (e.g. commercial and sport fishery; furs; recreation) | public prices; marginal productivity value; market pricing; participation models with unit-day recreational values; hedonic pricing; travel cost models; and contingent valuation | Lynne et al. (1981); Batie and Wilson (1979); Gupta and Foster (1975); Park and Batie (1979); Costanza et al. (1989); Mendelssohn et al. (1983); Thibodeau and Ostro (1981); Brown and Pollakowski (1977); Bishop and Heberlein (1980); Costanza et al. (1989); Farber and Costanza (1989) |
| **Indirect (functional) benefits** (flood control; treatment; groundwater recharge; waste atmospheric and life-support functions) | damage cost avoided analysis; alternative/ substitute costs; and energy efficiency analysis | Gosselink et al. (1974); Costanza et al. (1989); Gupta and Foster (1975); Tchobanoglous and Culp (1980); Fritz and Helle (1979); Williams (1980); Thibodeau and Ostro (1981); Kahn and Kemp (1985); Constanza et al. (1989); Farber and Costanza (1989)[11] |
| **Option value and non-use value** | contingent valuation models | Costanza, Farber and Maxwell (1989); Farber and Costanza (1987)[12] |
| *Useful supplementary data:* | | |
| **Forgone development output value** (agricultural output; recreational housing) | opportunity cost models | Turner et al. (1983); Batie and Shabman (1982); Shabman et al. (1979); Batie and Mabbs-Zeno (1985); Shabman and Bertlesen (1979); Turner (1988 a and b); Bowers (1983)[13] |

not enough to base wetland management decisions on existing use values.

In the next section, we discuss some of the problems that such a narrow approach has created in the past.

## Sources of inefficiency in wetland-resource use

### *Historical land-use conflict loss*

Given the favourable location of most wetlands – along rivers; on coasts; and on level terrain, often with inherently fertile soils – pressure on wetlands is inevitable as the economic development process intensifies. The fact that wetlands are so attractive for a wide range of economic activities means that a "natural" process of conflict is inherent to wetlands. For example, coastal and estuarine wetlands have suffered substantial losses because of agricultural reclamation, urban and industrial development, and recreation use pressures. Over time, many wetland sites have been lost, as economies have industrialized and their agricultural sectors have become more intensive. As explained above, much of this historical loss does not necessarily represent "inefficient" resource use. This is particularly so in developing countries, where the multiple use of wetlands can lead to significant improvements in social welfare.

### *Information, market and intervention failures*

Three types of "failure" phenomena can be identified as playing an important role in this process:

(i) **information failures** – a general lack of appreciation of the full economic value of conserved wetlands, which has contributed to subsequent market and intervention failures;
(ii) **market failures** – in particular, wetlands have suffered from pollution (externality problem); and from water supply diminution as a result of excessive abstraction of open-access water resources (public good failure). Another form of the externality problem occurs when

wetland benefits do not accrue to the wetland owner, resulting in a divergence between private and social benefits

(iii) **intervention failures** – the general absence of properly integrated resource-management policies has resulted in intersectoral policy inconsistencies and wetland degradation. There are also examples of inefficient policies directed at wetlands themselves, and of policies directed at other sectoral issues which carried with them unintended "spill-over" effects for wetlands.

Table 1.2 summarizes the typical intervention and market failures identified in the case studies. The most ubiquitous form of *market failure* encountered was that of externalities. All types of wetlands have suffered, to a greater or lesser extent, from externalities. This has resulted in pollution damage, from both on- and off-site pollution sources. Industrial and agricultural pollution, in some instances combined with sewerage effluent, have served in subtle and complicated ways to degrade the chemical and biological quality of wetlands. In the majority of cases, water-borne pollution has been the main problem, but some upland wetlands have also suffered from air pollution in the form of acid deposition. The degradation process usually results in a series of latent-damage impacts, including the loss of species diversity. Saltmarshes, coastal marshes and intertidal mudflats are also all at risk from climate change-induced sea level rise.

The run-off of agricultural chemicals and soil erosion (increased sedimentation) have combined with point-source pollution from effluent treatment plants to inflict serious damage on estuarine wetlands, such as Chesapeake Bay, USA. Similar problems have occurred in the Norfolk Broadland in the UK and elsewhere in Europe. Other wetlands have been degraded by industrial effluent flowing to watercourses which subsequently flow through, or near, wetlands. The Po delta wetlands in Italy, for example, have been heavily polluted in this way.

Because these pollution-induced changes are often only latent, and do not (in the short run) result in obvious physical changes, they pose particularly difficult management problems. Therefore, it is likely that most existing estimates of wetland

**Table 1.2: A typology of intervention and market failures**

| | |
|---|---|
| **Market failures** | |
| 1. *Pollution externalities* | |
| (a) air pollution, off-site | excess levels of sulphur and nitrogen causing loss species diversity |
| (b) water pollution, off-site | excess nitrogen and phosphorous from sewerage and agricultural sources; some industrial (toxic) pollution |
| (c) water pollution, on-site | agricultural and recreational pressures |
| 2. *Public goods-type problem* | |
| (a) ground-water depletion/ surface-water supply diminution | overexploitation on- and off-site of wetlands water supply |
| (b) congestion costs, on-site | recreation pressure on wetland carrying cacity. |
| **Intervention failures** | |
| 3. *Intersectoral policy inconsistency* | |
| (a) competing sector output prices | agricultural price fixing and associated land requirements. |
| (b) competing sector input prices | tax breaks or outmoded tax categories on agricultural land; or tax breaks for housing or industrial usage; tax breaks on forestry capital; low interest loans to farmers; conversion subsidies; (drainage, fill, flood protection, flood insurance); subsidies on other agricultural inputs and on research and development biased towards intensive farming methods |
| (c) land-use policy | zoning; regional development policy; direct conversion of wetlands policy; agricultural set-aside schemes; waste disposal policy |
| 4. *Counterproductive wetlands policy* | |
| (a) inefficient policy | e.g. policies that lack a long-term structure |
| (b) institutional failure | lack of monitoring and survey capacity, and information dissemination; non-integrative agencies structure |

loss rates undervalue the true rate of ongoing degradation, because they are limited to the observation of physical changes.

In regions which possess relatively dry climates, wetlands have been especially damaged because of their "public good" character, for example open-access to scarce water resources. Open-access has led to surface-water supply losses to wetlands, as well as to groundwater supply depletion. For example, in Spain (e.g. Daimiel National Park; the Laguna de las Salinas and the Laguna de la Celadilla), the continuous exploitation of a limited water supply, mainly for irrigated agriculture, has led to surface drying in wetland areas, and fears that the groundwater resource is itself being depleted.

The failure to account for conservation values (especially the "non-use" aspects of this value) may also represent a failure to meet the intergenerational efficiency objective. For example, if the infilling of a wetland represents its permanent removal, this may represent a denial of an opportunity for future generations to benefit from wetland services.

From the wetlands-resource management viewpoint, the key factor here is that, in the presence of such "publicness", markets will supply too little wetland conservation. Again, the need for appropriate policy intervention is highlighted.

Where wetlands supply recreational opportunities, these goods/services are examples of "congestible" goods. There is the danger that utilization levels might result in overcrowding and subsequent reductions in resource quality, as the wetland area's "carrying capacity" is exceeded. In the case of "congestible" goods, exclusion results in efficient use only if the actual consumers pay for their use in accordance with their real willingness to pay. There are, however, usually obstacles (e.g. high costs) both to collecting such payments, and to finding out the true willingness to pay of these consumers. Nevertheless, some exclusion-type management devices are often possible. In the Norfolk Broads, for example, recreation pressure, in terms of boating activities, is partially regulated by limits on the number of boat licences issued.

The absence of enforceable property rights related to wetland conservation benefits means that farmers, for example, have little incentive to protect wetlands against actions that would diminish their supply (or to take action that would increase their supply). Property rights are poorly developed, either because of difficulties controlling access to the wetland service, or because the value of this service is less than the cost of controlling access to it.

The *intervention failure* category is a complicated one, and is, in most cases, linked to both information and market failures. It should also be recognized that it is sometimes difficult to say conclusively what constitutes an intervention failure. Historically, a large number of wetland conversions in the developed economies probably did represent socially beneficial resource-allocation decisions. These conversions, for example, led to much-needed increases in agricultural output, and to reduced threats to human health at the time. The same general argument is probably applicable to some wetland conversions in the developing economies.

Many examples exist of inefficient policies aimed specifically at wetlands. The Spanish Water Act of 1879 (valid until 1985) included a provision which classified lagoons and shallow-water environments as "unhealthy areas". Tax deductions and other economic incentives were made available to encourage the drainage and reclamation of such areas – especially in the period after 1950. But this policy had the effect of classifying all wetlands as "unhealthy", and therefore stimulated an inefficient, in this case excessive, level of wetland conversion.

Some policies attempting to foster the sustainable usage of wetlands have proved to be inefficient because they lacked a long enough time horizon. Thus, the introduction of relatively low-intensity fish-farming in some French wetlands initially served to keep the wetlands and their reedbeds intact. But new technology for reed-cutting, and subsidies for intensive fish-farming, now pose a significant threat to the long-term survival of the wetlands.

Developing countries have also suffered from inefficient wetland policies. In peninsular Malaysia, for example, many freshwater swamps have been drained for rice cultivation. But yields have been disappointing because the fields have lacked a regular supply of fresh water. This supply was traditionally supplied by the swamps. Overall, in developed and developing economies, sustainable development represents a fragile balance between technology, economics and environmental conservation.

The absence of nationally-integrated resource-management

policies has also resulted in intervention failures. This failure takes the form of intersectoral policy inconsistency,which leads to wetland destruction or degradation. The interface between agricultural conversion and intensification policy on the one hand, and wetland conservation, especially lowland freshwater types, conservation on the other, is the most ubiquitous example of this type of intervention failure.

Saline soil marshes in the UK, France and Holland, as well as interior wetlands – northern prairie potholes and southern bottomland hardwood forested wetlands – in North America, have suffered particularly high losses due to conversion to high intensity agriculture. The agricultural conversion process has been artificially stimulated by a range of subsidies, price guarantees and tax incentives given to farmers.

In both Europe and the USA, farmers have often been subsidized to drain and convert wetlands and traditional grazing marshes into arable cropping land. For example, in France between 10 per cent and 60 per cent of the costs of field drainage, ditches and channels have historically been paid out of public funds. Until the mid-1980s, the UK Ministry of Agriculture, Fisheries and Food (MAFF) operated a system of drainage grants to help farmers convert land, including wetlands, to higher-productivity crops.

However, the real driving force behind the conversion of wetlands in Europe has been the high general level of intervention prices paid for a number of crops under the EEC's Common Agricultural Policy (CAP). Under the CAP, intervention prices for cereals have at certain times been well above world market prices, for instance, EEC wheat prices were 40–60 per cent above world market prices over the period 1978–80. The effect of this policy has been to make the conversion of lowland wet grazing meadows a very profitable financial investment for individual farmers.

Several other intersectoral policy inconsistency situations are provided in the case studies. Three specific examples are listed below.

(i) Forestry policies leading to the destruction of blanket bogs in the UK. Globally-scarce blanket bogs in Caithness and Sutherland in Scotland are now under severe threat from coniferous afforestation.

(ii) Publicly-funded dams for water storage and hydroelectric power generators can lead to wetland destruction. Examples are the South Hainberg riverine forest wetland controversy in Austria, and the loss of a number of wetlands in France.

(iii) Regional-aid policies in the European Community have led, in both France and Greece, to the establishment of intensive fish-farming enterprises. These activities have sometimes polluted the surrounding wetlands, and led to the abandonment of traditional (sustainable) management activities in the wetlands.

## *Towards a sustainable wetland economy*

Effective wetland management at the national level will typically depend upon a careful inventory of the range of wetlands that exists in each country; of the functions and services which these wetlands provide; of their capacity to support extensive and intensive management; and of the economic value of their use and non-use benefits. Figure 1.3 illustrates an "idealized" progression from the original identification of management failure to reach the eventual goal of sustainable management. Obviously, each step in figure 1.3 implies a large interdisciplinary research effort. Furthermore, in implementing this "ideal" model, it is important to understand the different "wetland contexts" that exist.

For example, in North America, and other relatively low population/large land-mass economies, an extensive network of natural and semi-natural wetlands still exists. The scope for "wilderness preservation" policies, although more limited now than in the past, is still considerable. Contrast this situation with that in Europe, where most, if not all, of the wetland ecosystems and landscapes are semi-natural. Most European wetlands have been created or modified by human activities. Modern-day land use pressures are also greater in Europe.

In addition, the resource constraints on research in developing countries, coupled with the imminent nature of the threat of conversion facing large tracts of tropical wetlands, both suggest that wetland management in these countries will have to emphasize quick action with a certain loss of analytical precision.

**Figure 1.3: Sustainable management of wetlands**

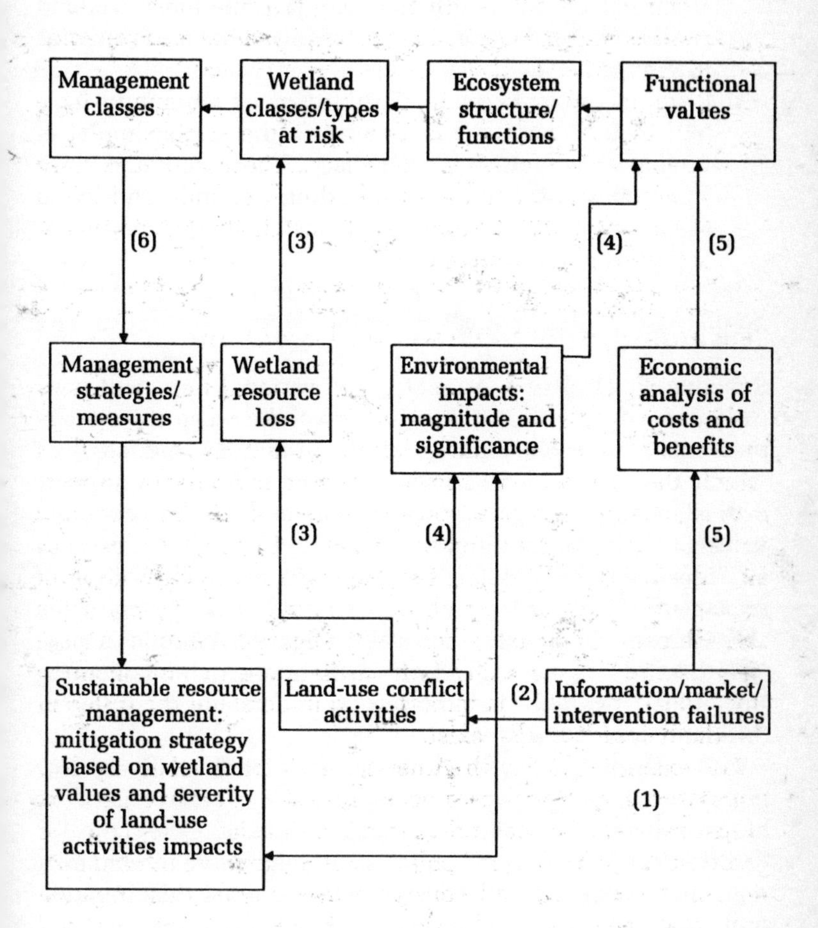


Source: Pearce and Turner (1990).

Different physical wetland contexts between countries are reinforced by political and cultural differences. Thus, it is likely that a wide array of policy instruments (regulatory and non-regulatory) will be required in any wetland conservation strategy, and that the precise mix of instruments and institutions, at the national level, will vary from country to country. Table 1.3 lists the basic management measures that are available, from which such choices will typically be made.

## *Sustainable wetland management in Europe*

In Europe, it is likely that there will have to be relatively more emphasis on policies aimed at sustainable use, rather than on nature reserve acquisition and conservation alone. In this context, sustainability must be seen as a process of balanced change guided by economic incentives and regulations, for example Environmentally Sensitive Area (ESA) designation. In other words, wetland protection strategies need to be more comprehensive than just protecting threatened species and establishing reserves. This is not to reject the concept of nature reserves, but to emphasize the need for this policy option to be reinforced.

The extensive semi-natural wetlands which exist in Europe can only be conserved if appropriate management rules and incentive structures can be applied. The challenge is to find practical "environmentally benign" economic activities which will be compatible with the sustainable utilization of wetlands.

The insidious problem of wetland degradation due to pollution (market failure) will require a more consistent and probably more rigorous application of the Polluter Pays Principle, via pollution taxes, permits, and/or regulations.

Greater integration in pollution control policy would also serve to enhance wetland protection. This integration can be interpreted in at least three ways:

(i) *spatial integration* – non-point source pollution and cross-media pollution remain pervasive problems in all OECD economies. There is a need to move beyond an examination of pollution only at the source, and to consider impacts across a wider geographical area. Policies regulating water

## Table 1.3: Wetland management policy instrument options

| Policy instruments | | | Comments |
|---|---|---|---|
| 1. *Regulation* | | | |
| | prohibitions | | To regulate wetland uses and |
| | | | encourage impact mitigation, |
| Planning | | | with or without compensation. |
| designations | zoning and – | subject to | National, regional or local |
| | designation | licence/ | permits with uniform |
| | | permit | conditions. |
| | permissions | | Zoning and designation of |
| | | | wetlands by permitted use |
| | | | or activity; UK SSSIs, nature |
| | specific | | reserves, national/regional |
| | controls | | parks, global biospherical |
| | over land – | subject to | abatement reserves (Ramsar |
| Pollution | use | licence/ | Convention); varying degrees |
| abatement | | permit | of site protection in practice. |
| | ambient | | |
| | quality | | |
| | standards | | |
| | | | Increased stringency in |
| | | | pollution control policy; |
| | | | ambient environmental quality. |
| 2. *Acquisition and management* | | | |
| | public body | | |
| Purchase | | | |
| | charitable – | covenants | |
| | body with | | |
| | public grant | | |
| | aid | | |
| Leasehold | –via covenant– | by owner | |
| | with | | |
| | management – | by accredited agent | |
| Management agreement – | | with landowner | |
| | | subject to agreement | |
| 3. *Incentives and charges* | | | |
| | ESAs; | | |
| | management | | |
| Subsidies | agreements | | |
| conservation | | | |
| management | Compensation | | |
| | for wetland, | | |

continued

**Table 1.3: Wetland management policy instrument options (continued)**

| Policy instruments | | Comments |
|---|---|---|
| | wildlife, crop damage; conservation practices (headlands hedgerows, etc.) | |
| Tax incentives for conservation management | on land<br>on inputs and other costs | Income, capital gains and estate tax exemptions for protected wetlands; deductions or credits on wetland donations or sales for conservation; property tax relief for protected wetlands. |
| Wetland loss mitigation charges | | Wetland development fees and related public trust fund for conservation; mitigation land banks (unadulterated or restored wetlands). |
| User charges | entrance fees<br>licences | Wetland hunting, fishing licence fees; non-consumption use licences; recreation entrance fees. |
| Development activity subsidies | agriculture, road construction, recreational, housing, forestry etc. | Removal or reduction in scope/extent e.g. of agricultural subsidies including drainage and irrigation cost sharing, loans, crop flood insurance, commodity price supports; tax deductions for development costs. |

*Source*: Pearce and Turner (1990).

pollution and waste disposal, for example, can also serve to protect wetlands from chemical and biological changes;

(ii) *administrative and institutional integration* – the institutional frameworks necessary to support wetland policy need to cover all environmental media;

(iii) *analytical and data integration* – the concept of "total economic value" needs to be applied to all forms of natural capital, including wetlands. In a practical project appraisal context, there is a need to improve the integration of environmental impact assessment with the standard economic cost-benefit approach. Project appraisal should be seen as an ongoing and anticipatory process which includes all of the following stages:

- pre-project environmental assessment;
- pre-project benefit-cost analysis;
- post-project environmental impact assessment;
- post-project economic appraisal and feedback mechanisms.

All European countries are signatories to the International Ramsar Convention, and a large number of estuarine wetlands have been designated as Ramsar Sites. Many European estuaries have also been designated as Specially Protected Areas under the European Community Directive on the Conservation of Wild Birds (EC 79/409).

Member countries of the European Community all have the capability to designate "environmentally sensitive areas". This concept has its origin in EEC Regulation No. 797/85, introduced in March 1985, as part of a package of measures designed to mitigate the twin problems of farm income maintenance and surplus production. Under Article 19(9) of the Regulation, it is possible to identify "areas of recognized importance from ecological and landscape points of view". Member states may make available grant-aid to farmers who undertake to farm environmentally important areas so as to preserve or improve the environment. Regulation No. 797/85 is, nevertheless, primarily a means of persuading farmers to reduce agricultural production, rather than a conservation measure in itself.

By 1989, for example, some 13 ESAs had been established in

the UK and many of these areas are also important wetlands. The UK ESA scheme offers financial incentives to farmers who follow a set of management guidelines designed to promote traditional low intensity land-uses. They discourage the conversion of land to arable regimes – which require deep drainage – in favour of low-intensity summer grazing regimes – usually due to high water tables. In this way, both the landscape and ecology aspects of wetlands can potentially be conserved on a sustainable use basis.

The main drawback of ESA-type schemes, at least, as presently set up in the UK, is that the incentive payments, and the farming practices they encourage, cover only a limited period of time (e.g. five years). There is a clear need for such schemes to be extended to cover the long-term conservation needs of wetlands.

Many conservation bodies have also spent large sums of money on the conservation of wetlands, using purchase and acquisition strategies. The "purchase" policy has the advantage of overcoming the property rights problem. However, in Europe, with its much diminished wetlands stock and the heavily transformed nature of many of its remaining wetlands, the purchase option is no panacea. Both the fragmented nature of the wetlands stock and the present ownership pattern of many wetland areas complicate matters considerably. Establishing a viable, that is, large enough, wetland reserve by purchase or lease will often take considerable time in Europe.

The problem of establishing wetland reserves of an adequate size is further complicated by the "open-system" nature of wetland ecosystems. Even the formal establishment, via legislation, of protected wetland park areas, fulfills only some of the requirements for conservation to occur. Thus, although the establishment of the Coto de Doñana National Park Wetland in Spain was a step in the right direction, the fact that the complete wetland ecosystem is not encompassed within the park boundaries means that the protected area can still be affected by activities considerable distances away from the park itself.

## *Sustainable wetland management in North America*

The United States has adopted several different remedial measures that attempt to address both market failure and intervention failures. However, empirical data to evaluate the effectiveness of these measures is not yet readily available.

Policies to acquire farmland of high habitat value are in place in the USA and Canada. These countries have agreed to acquire several million acres of wetlands in the northern plains of the USA and the adjacent prairie region of Canada. Wetlands in these areas are of major importance as habitat for waterfowl and other animals. The objective of this North American Waterfowl Management Plan (NAWMP) is to preserve some of the habitat values of these lands against further agricultural conversion.

So far, the resources available to conservation bodies have only been adequate to purchase a small proportion of the land under threat of drainage. The NAWMP – the most extensive example of the wetland-purchase policy in action which yet exists – calls for the acquisition of only five or six million acres of wetlands in an area where the total wetland acreage is in the order of tens of millions.

Nevertheless, purchase, unlike some other policy options, does represent a long-term wetland conservation approach. Over the next few decades, policies aimed at expanding purchasing activities by both public and private agencies in North America could go some way toward overcoming the property-rights obstacles to increasing the supply of wetland conservation values in agriculture.

Three types of regulatory programmes have typically been used in North America to control wetland conversions. The first type is directed at the wetlands themselves, and generally limits (or prohibits) certain types of alterations to the resource directly, for example infilling or drainage. The second type controls activities that may alter wetland industry indirectly. For instance, a regulation that requires a hydroelectric facility to obtain a government licence before it can be built may prohibit the responsible agency from issuing the licence when significant conversion of wetlands would result.

The third type of regulation focuses on the functional values of wetlands, particularly on their importance in providing wildlife habitat for certain species. These regulations limit proposed alterations if they would significantly interfere with these values.

Overall, North American experience suggests that market incentive measures – taxes or subsidies – will have to be combined with legislation which establishes conservation zones (e.g. ESAs), if extensive enough areas of wetland are to be protected on a long-term basis. Some analysts have suggested that an assurance-bonding system could be established in order to get prospective developers and other parties responsible for wetland loss/damage into an economic trade-off situation. The idea is that parties responsible for wetland destruction would be charged the full social cost involved in their action, that is, the estimated total economic value of conserved wetlands per acre. The fees collected would go into an assurance bond, which would be returned to the developers in the event that damages were less than the worst-case estimate assumed in the fee calculation. Alternatively, the fees could be applied to wetland loss mitigation schemes elsewhere in the region (Costanza, Farber and Maxwell, 1989).

Such an approach would provide a strong economic incentive for developers and/or polluters to seek out impact-minimization options, as well as to fund research into the functional values of wetlands, in order to test the scientific validity of the "worst-case" calculation, on which the fee would be based.

## *Wetland management in developing countries*

As discussed earlier, sustainable utilization and the maintenance of a sustainable flow of income from the wetlands stock are the key priorities for developing economies.

The open-system nature of wetlands means that an "extensive approach" to management will usually be required. Long-term, integrated river basin management strategies co-ordinated with national water resource and wetland policies will therefore be needed. The difficulty of meeting this need in developing countries cannot be overestimated. International river basins harbour many of the developing world's major wetlands, and depend upon these wetlands for many of their basic characteristics. For example, 60 per cent of African and South American wetland areas are found in such river basins. The figure for Asia is 65 per cent.

The difficulties involved in devising a sustainable wetland management policy in the developing country context are well illustrated by the case of the Hadejia-Nguru wetlands in Nigeria (Adams and Hollis, 1988). These wetlands cover an area of

30 000 ha, and represent seasonally damp or flooded land under the influence of the Hadejia and Jama' are rivers.

The total economic value of the Hadejia-Nguru floodplain area has, for centuries, been based on the traditional exploitation of the natural capital, for example flood agriculture, small-scale irrigation, fishing, grazing and hunting. The flood plain supports a large population, while still producing a surplus for trade. The economic significance of the area is increasing over time, particularly as drought increasingly affects the northern regions of Nigeria. The floodplain is also of high nature-conservation value.

The rivers servicing the area lose flows as a result of evaporation, transpiration and the infiltration of river water into the Chad aquifer. Since the early 1970s, there has also been a general shortage of rainfall throughout the Sahelian zone, which has resulted in reduced flooding and a general shortage of water. These reductions could have serious negative implications, both for traditional wetland activities and for the supporting ecology. The floodplain also provides important dry season pastures which are used by nomadic peoples. Conflicts are now developing over access to flooded areas, as dry-season agriculture intensifies.

The risk of drought has been further increased by water resource decisions taken in the 1970s. Dams, large-scale irrigation and water-basin transfer schemes devised by river-basin development authorities and state ministries were designed on the basis of hydrologic data from the relatively wet period up to 1973.

Plans were also poorly co-ordinated, resulting in the construction of high capital-cost, low net-benefit projects (intervention failure). Because of capital-budget constraints, some of these schemes were only partially completed.

The increasingly drought-prone region still lacks a coherent water resource plan. Proposed dam construction projects at Katin Zaki and Challawa Gorge would permit an operating regime sufficient to service some large- and small-scale pump irrigation, but could only be accomplished at the expense of the floodplain wetlands system.

Devising a sustainable management regime for the area is a complex task. Economic activities in the floodplain are closely integrated. Different households in the same village may use different economic strategies – farming, grazing and fishing – at different times, as their resource endowment and external conditions change. As we have already highlighted, access to, and rights over, grazing and other resources has generated conflict. This is typical of open-access, multi-use resource systems. The economy of the floodplain is dynamic, and is constantly reacting to a combination of natural, legal, and economic changes.

Floodplain economic activities are, of course, fundamentally interrelated with the ecosystems of the area. Ecological conservation is a vital element in any sustainable development strategy. In the case of Hadejia-Nguru floodplain, zoning is the most likely way of achieving this goal. Some combination of nature reserves, buffer zones and sustainable utilization of the rest of the floodplain is required, but it will not be easy to ensure.

As the Hadejia-Nguru wetlands example illustrates, the *sustainable-use* objective cannot be neglected in the developing economy context, although the *conservation* of the highest natural and structural wetland values should also often be a high national priority. In developing economies, this conservation could have a high opportunity cost. If the Hadejia-Nguru wetlands are to be conserved, key areas must be designated as strictly managed natural reserves. But this approach would have to be combined with compensatory and other sustainable development options both in buffer zones and elsewhere on the floodplain.

## *Sustainable development and the notion of substitutability*

Offsetting the physical loss and degradation of wetlands via a "no-net-loss" policy has much to recommend it. This policy goal need not be interpreted in terms of absolute limits. The key issue here is the nature and extent of potential substitution opportunities.

We can examine the opportunities for substitution in terms of the different classes of wetlands. For example, "internationally important" wetlands can be seen as elements of the stock of "critical" natural capital. These assets are characterized by essentiality, irreversibility and uncertainty. The essentiality characteristic ensures a high total economic value, and also corresponds to a low or zero degree of substitutability. Such resources should be subject to an anticipatory and precautionary, safe minimum standards (SMS) approach. Conditions of irreversibility and uncertainty reinforce a policy prescription in favour of wetland conservation rather than development. Available evidence suggests that, for this "critical" wetland type, the SMS has already been reached.

In order to conserve such high-value wetlands, international action is required, because it will often be necessary to retain physically large tracts of habitats. Thus, the support system for migratory birds comprises several types of ecosystems, many of which are physically separated by thousands of miles. Other high-value wetlands provide extended food-web services or are linked to global climatic mechanisms (carbon sources and sinks). Conservation of such globally important resources must be a high priority. International conventions and global biospherical reserve designation (as advocated by the Brundtland Commission) are among the options which will need to be examined in this context.

Relatively lower-value wetlands could be treated as components of the "other natural capital" stock, and as such, may be substituted for by man-made capital. In these cases, degradation or depletion can be accepted if sufficient assets are substituted in place of the original wetland. This implies that "shadow projects" – wetland restoration and/or artificial creation – will have to be included in any plan to degrade natural wetlands. The shadow projects must fully compensate for the wetland loss wrought by the other projects in the portfolio. The shadow-project options should be as cost-effective as possible, but should *not* be subject to the normal cost-benefit efficiency rules.

The extent to which habitat loss can be compensated for, by creating "new" semi-natural areas closely resembling the lost asset is a complex question. Based on limited fieldwork experience to date, there are three reconstruction options available (Buckley, 1989):

(i) *habitat reconstruction* – the construction of ecological communities away from the site being lost because of the development activity;

(ii) *habitat transplantation* – moving a habitat away from the donor site to a receptor site; and
(iii) *habitat restoration* – enhancing the ecological potential of existing but degraded or impoverished habitats of the same type as that threatened by development.

The habitat construction option could involve extending the threatened habitat, for example deliberate flooding of extra land close to the original wetland site, or allowing flora and fauna to colonize over time (also known as "habitat duplication"). On the other hand, artificially-created habitats may be located some distance from the development site. The danger in this approach is that no site is ever totally isolated from its surroundings. For this reason, small isolated parcels of conserved habitats are unlikely to remain viable in biodiversity terms over the long term.

There are at least two types of habitat reconstruction policy modes:

(i) to create relatively simple habitats, or habitats providing only a limited number of functional services, for example bird nesting or wintering areas; and
(ii) the "strong" conservation option to recreate the most convincing replicas of ancient and complex habitats that it is technically possible to achieve.

Conservationists would argue that the "strong" option could best be operationalized by a strategy that was committed to retaining *all* existing semi-natural habitats. For example, despite the existence of some twenty conservation designations stemming from 30 Acts of Parliament in the UK, important landscape and ecological sites (including wetlands) continue to be lost. The next component of the strategy would be the "duplication" of ecological communities centred around existing Sites of Special Scientific Interest (SSSI) and National Nature Reserve (NNR). Finally, attempts could be made to recreate appropriate habitats related to biogeographical regions (Buckley, 1989).

Adequate substitutes may not be available because of either physical or financial constraints. In these instances, the net costs or benefits of imposing conservation standards can be represented by the net benefits of the potential forgone development project(s). The decision-maker will then have to decide whether or not the imposition of the environmental constraint is worth the cost.

It may also be possible to augment the supply of lower-order wetlands by constructing new artificial wetlands, or by reclaiming, or more intensively managing, existing areas. Current marsh-establishment technology may be expected to play a role in this process. However, recent experience in both Britain and Holland indicates that restoration will be a protracted and expensive affair. Although considerable success has been achieved in restoring small areas of the Norfolk Broads in the UK, extensive use of this approach in multiple-use wetlands is clearly not a practical proposition.

Overall, it seems reasonable to conclude that most wetlands, once destroyed, can be only partially and imperfectly replaced by man. Since most outright wetland development decisions are irreversible, in both physical and economic terms, a strong case exists for wetland conservation in the first place. This conclusion is based on both economic efficiency and intergenerational equity grounds.

## Summary

Evidence from all the case studies indicates that market and intervention failures have led to the loss of wetlands in most countries. The most obvious problem has been the systematic conversion of wetlands to other uses: agricultural, industrial and recreational. More subtle and complex quality declines have also been inflicted on wetlands by both air and water pollution.

Wetlands represent very valuable natural capital assets and therefore require conservation and sustainable management. A "no-net-loss" policy approach offers considerable promise in this regard. This policy objective need not be interpreted in terms of absolute limits. For some classes of wetlands, substitution opportunities may be available.

Furthermore, there is a need to strike a balance between outright wetland conservation and sustainable usage of the wetland. A range of mitigative and remedial policies are required, tailored to suit different national circumstances. Many countries have already enacted measures intended to halt, or at least to slow down, wetland losses. Empirical evidence pertaining to the precise success or failure of these measures is not yet available. However, policy successes have probably been "patchy", depending on the country involved.

With the exception of the wetland-purchase policy, most of the other policy options provide only short-term conservation protection. More extensive purchasing of wetlands is likely to yield major social benefits in those regions (e.g. North America) where relatively extensive, and remote, wetlands still exist. In regions where wetlands are already much transformed (e.g. Europe), the purchase option will be more difficult to use, but it may still offer some scope for achieving increased conservation. Sustainable usage and co-operative management systems will be the norm in most European countries. A promising start has been made with the introduction of the ESA concept. But this approach needs to be refined, made more extensive, and above all, put on a long-term basis.

Finally, sustainable usage will be the key requirement for tropical wetlands in developing countries. In this context, globally-significant wetland resources will require biospheric reserve designation, or similar status. To make such designations operational, there will be a need for international compensatory resource transfers – for example debt for nature swaps and/or other devices – to aid developing economies.

The case studies presented in the remainder of this book discuss the state of wetlands in four OECD countries and review the market and intervention failures that exist in each. A review of these case studies reveals much to be apprehensive about for the future of wetlands. However, it also reveals much to be hopeful about. It is on these hopes that future management policies must build.

## References

Adams, W. M. and G. E. Hollis, *Hydrology and Sustainable Resource Development of a Sahelian Floodplain Wetland* (London: University College, 1988).

Barbier, E. B., *Economic Evaluation of Tropical Wetland Resources*

*Application in Central America*. LEEC Working Paper (London: University College, 1989).

Batie, S. S. and C. C. Mabbs-Zeno, "Opportunity Costs of Preserving Coastal Wetlands: A Case Study of a Recreational Housing Development", *Land Economics*, vol. 61, no. 1 (1985).

Batie, S. S. and L. Shabman, "Estimating The Economic Value of Wetlands: Principles, Methods and Limitations", *Coastal Zone Management Journal*, vol. 10, no. 3 (1982).

Batie, S. S. and J. R. Wilson, *Economic Values Attributable to Virginia's Coastal Wetlands and Inputs in Oyster Production*. Research Division Bulletin 150, Dept. of Agricultural Economics (Blacksberg: Virginia Polytechnic Institute and State University, 1979).

Bishop, R. and T. A. Heberlein, *Simulated Markets, Hypothetical Markets and Travel Cost Analysis: Alternative Methods of Estimating Outdoor Recreation Demand*. Dept. of Agricultural Economics Staff Paper 187 (University of Wisconsin, 1980).

Brown, G. M. and H. O. Pollakowski, "Economic Valuation of Shoreline", *Review of Economics and Statistics*, vol. 59 (1977).

Bowers, J. K., "Cost Benefit Analysis of Wetland Drainage", *Environment and Planning*, vol. 15, no. 2 (1983).

Bowers, J. K., "Cost Benefit Analysis in Theory and Practice: Agricultural Land Drainage Projects", in Turner, R. K., *Sustainable Environmental Management: Principles and Practice* (London: Belhaven Press, 1988).

Buckley, G. P. (ed.), *Biological Habitat Reconstruction* (London: Belhaven Press, 1989).

Costanza, R., S. Farber and J. Maxwell, "Valuation and Management of Wetland Ecosystems", *Ecological Economics*, 1, pp.335–61 (1989).

Cowan, J. H., R. E. Turner and D. R. Cahoon, "Marsh Management Plans in Practice: Do They Work in Coastal Louisiana, U.S.A?" *Environmental Management*, vol. 12, no. 1 (1988).

Crosson, P. R., *Supplying the Environmental Values of Agriculture* RFF Paper No. 98, Washington DC (1990).

Dixon, J. A., "Valuation of Mangroves", *Tropical Coastal Area Management*, vol. 4 (1989).

Dossor, J., *Land Drainage Improvement Scheme for Five Mile Level: A Consulting Report* (Norwich: Dossor and Partners, 1984).

Farber, S. and R. Costanza, "The Economic Value of Wetland Systems", *Journal of Environmental Management*, vol. 24, pp.41–51 (1989).

Freeman, A. M., "The Quasi-Option Value of Irreversible Development", *Journal of Environmental Economics and Management*, vol. 11, no. 3 (1984).

Fisher, A. C. and W. M. Haverman, "Endangered Species: The Economics of Irreversible Damage", in Hall, D. *et al.* (eds), *Economics of Ecosystem Management* (Dordrecht: W. Junk Publishers, 1985).

Fritz, W. R. and S. C. Helle, "Cypress Wetlands for Tertiary Treatment", in *Aquaculture Systems for Wastewater Treatment: Seminar Proceedings and Engineering Assessment*. USEPA Office of Water Programme Operations (Washington DC: Series Water 430/9-80-006, 1979).

Goodland, R. and G. Ledec, "Wildlands: Balancing Conversion with Conservation in World Bank Projects", *Environment*, vol. 31, pp.6–11, 27–35 (1989).

Gosselink, J. G., E. P. Odum and R. M. Pope, *The Value of the Tidal Marsh, Centre for Wetland Resources* (Baton Rouge: Louisiana State University, 1974).

Gupta, T. R. and J. H. Foster, "Economic Criteria for Freshwater Wetland Policy in Massachusetts", *American Journal of Agricultural Economics*, vol. 57, no. 1 (1975).

Kahn, J. R. and W. M. Kemp, "Economic Losses Associated with the Degradation of an Ecosystem: The Case of Submerged Aquatic Vegetation in Chesapeake Bay", *Journal of Environmental Economics and Management*, vol. 12, no. 3 (1985).

Lynne, G. D., P. Conray and F. J. Prochaska, "Economic Valuation of Marsh Areas for Marine Production Processes", *Journal of Environmental Economics and Management*, vol. 8, no. 2 (1981).

Mendelssohn, I. A., R. E. Turner and K. L. McKee, "Louisiana's Eroding Coastal Zone: Management Alternatives", *Journal of the Limnological Society of South Africa*, vol. 9, no. 2 (1983).

Milon, J. W., J. Gressel and D. Mulkey, "Hedonic Amenity Valuation and Functional Form Specification", *Land Economics*, vol. 60, no. 4 (1984).

Nelson, R. W., "Wetlands Policy Crisis: United States and United Kingdom", *Agriculture Ecosystem and Environment*, vol. 18 (1986).

Nelson, R. W. and W. J. Logan, "Policy on Wetland Mitigation", *Environment International*, vol. 10, no. 1 (1984).

Pearce, D. W. and R. K. Turner, *Economics of Natural Resources and the Environment* (Hemel Hempstead: Harvester Wheatsheaf, 1990).

Pearce, D. W., A. Markandya and B. Barbier, *Blueprint for a Green Economy* (London: Earthscan Publications, 1989).

Pezzey, J., *Economic Analysis of Sustainable Growth and Sustainable Development* (Washington DC: World Bank, Environment Department Working Paper no. 15, 1989).

Park, W. M. and S. S. Batie, *Methodological Issues Associated with Estimation of the Economic Value of Coastal Wetlands in*

*Improving Water Quality*. Sea Grant Project Paper VPl-SG-79-O9, Dept. of Agricultural Economics (Blacksburg: Virginia Polytechnic Institute and State University, 1989).

Race, M. S., "Critique of Present Wetlands Mitigation Policies in the U.S.A. Based on an Analysis of Past Restoration Projects in San Francisco Bay", *Environmental Management*, vol. 9, no. 1 (1985).

Seller, C., J. R. Stoll and J. Chavas, "Validation of Empirical Measures of Welfare Change: A Comparison of Nonmarket Techniques", *Land Economics*, vol. 61, no. 2 (1985).

Shabman, L., S. Batie and C. Mabbs-Zeno, "The Economics of Wetland Preservation in Virginia", *Journal of the North Eastern Agricultural Economics Council*, vol. 8, no. 2 (1979).

Shabman, L. and Bertelsen, "The Use of Development Value Estimates for Coastal Wetland Permit Decisions", *Land Economics*, vol. 55, no. 2 (1979).

Tchobanoglous, G. and G. L. Culp, "Wetland Systems for Wastewater Treatment: An Engineering Assessment", in *Aquaculture Systems for Wastewater Treatment*: Seminar Proceedings and Engineering Assessment. USEPA Office of Water Programme Operations (Washington DC: Series Water 430/9-80-007, 1980).

Thibodeau, F. R. and B. D. Ostro, "An Economic Analysis of Wetland Protection", *Journal of Environmental Management*, vol. 12, no. 1 (1981).

Thomas, R., "Future Sea Level Rise and its Early Detection by Satellite Remote Sensing", in Titus, J. G. (ed.), "Effects of Changes in Stratospheric Ozone and Global Climate", *Sea Level Rise*, vol. 4, pp.19–36 (Washington DC: USEPA, 1986).

Turner, R. K. (ed.), *Sustainable Environmental Management: Principles and Practice* (London: Belhaven Press, 1988a).

Turner, R. K., "Wetland Conservation: Economics and Ethics", in Collard, D. *et al.* (eds), *Economics, Growth and Sustainable Environments* (London: Macmillan, 1988b).

Turner, R. K., "Economics and Wetland Management", *Ambio*, vol. 20, no. 2, pp.59–63 (1991).

Turner, R. K. and J. Brooke, "Management and Valuation of an Environmentally Sensitive Area: Norfolk Broadland Case Study", *Environmental Management*, vol. 12, no. 3 (1988).

Turner, R. K., D. Dent and R. D. Hey, "Valuation of the Environmental Impact of Wetland Flood Protection and Drainage Schemes", *Environment and Planning*, vol. 15, no. 4 (1983).

Turner, R. K., "Economics and Environmentally Sensitive Aid", *International Journal of Environmental Studies*, vol. 35, pp.39–50 (1989).

Turner, R. K., M. Kelly and R. Kay, *Cities at Risk* (London: BNA International, 1990).

US Office of Technology Assessment, *Wetlands, their Use and Regulation* (Washington DC, 1984).

Williams, T. C., "Wetlands Irrigation Aids Man and Nature", *Water and Wastes Engineering*, pp.28–31 (Nov. 1980).

Willis, K. G. and J. F. Benson, "Valuation of Wildlife: A Case Study of the Upper Teesdale Site of Special Scientific Interest and Comparison of Methods in Environmental Economics", in Turner, R. K. ed., *Sustainable Environmental Management: Principles and Practice* (London: Belhaven Press, 1988).

Willis, K. G., J. F. Benson and C. M. Saunders, "The Impact of Agricultural Policy on the Costs of Nature Conservation", *Land Economics*, vol. 64, pp.147–57 (1988).

World Commission on Environment and Development (WCED), *Our Common Future* (Oxford: Oxford University Press, 1987).

# 2

# THE UNITED STATES

Edwin Clark II

## Wetlands in the United States: an overview

The US Fish and Wildlife Service estimates that, as of the mid-1970s, the conterminous United States contained approximately ninety-nine million acres of wetlands (US Fish and Wildlife Service, 1983). These statistics do not include approximately fifty-eight million acres of marine and inland lake areas, which can also be considered wetlands, or over two hundred million acres of tundra and other wetlands located in Alaska and Hawaii (Office of Technology Assessment, 1984). Inland freshwater wetlands account for approximately ninety-five per cent of the total. The rest are coastal, saline areas.

Table 2.1 summarizes the amount of the different types of US wetlands estimated to have existed in the mid-1950s and the mid-1970s. The saltwater areas include both marine intertidal regions – areas that are alternately exposed and covered by tides, including splash zones – and estuarine intertidal regions. The "estuarine intertidal" category is further broken down by vegetation characteristics – non-vegetated, emergent vegetation, and forested and scrub/shrub. Palustrine wetlands are non-tidal wetlands other than those associated with lakes or impoundments, larger than 20 acres (called "lacustrine wetlands"), or those contained within a river channel (called "riverine wetlands"). Palustrine wetlands are further characterized according to their vegetation characteristics.

Wetlands in the United States provide the same types of functions and values that they do in other parts of the world.

For example, the biological productivity of wetlands sometimes exceeds that of the finest farmland. Wetlands sustain nearly one third of the nation's endangered and threatened wildlife species. They provide breeding and wintering grounds for millions of waterfowl and shore birds every year. Coastal wetlands provide nursery and spawning grounds for 60–90 per cent of US commercial fish catches. In spite of such obvious connections as the fact that coastal wetlands are important for providing habitat for marine fish, no rigorous effort has yet been made to associate the importance of different types of functions with different types of wetlands.

**Table 2.1: Wetland types, acreages and losses in the conterminous United States for selected years (in 000s of acres)**

| Type of wetland | Area in mid-1950s | Area in mid-1970s | Net loss | % Loss |
|---|---|---|---|---|
| **Marine intertidal** | 82.4 | 78.4 | 4.0 | 4.9 |
| **Estuarine intertidal** | | | | |
| non-vegetated | 741.1 | 746.5 | (5.4) | (0.8) |
| emergent | 4276.0 | 3922.8 | 353.2 | 8.3 |
| forested & shrub/scrub | 592.1 | 573.0 | 19.1 | 3.3 |
| *Subtotal* (estuarine intertidal) | 5609.2 | 5242.3 | 366.9 | 6.6 |
| **Palustrine** | | | | |
| non–vegetated | 2704.4 | 4970.5 | (2266.1) | (83.8) |
| forested | 55 707.4 | 49 713.4 | 5994.0 | 10.8 |
| scrub/shrub | 10 998.2 | 10 611.1 | 387.1 | 3.6 |
| emergent | 33 112.6 | 28 441.4 | 4671.2 | 14.4 |
| Subtotal (Palustrine) | 102 522.6 | 93 736.4 | 8786.2 | 8.6 |
| **Lacustrine** | 56 562.7 | 57 923.6 | (1360.9) | (2.5) |
| **Total (all types)** | 164 776.9 | 156 980.7 | 7796.2 | 4.8 |

Source: US Fish and Wildlife Service (1983)

Nor, in spite of numerous efforts, are meaningful figures available on the *value* of the functions that wetlands provide. The Wetlands Value Data Base, maintained by the US Fish and Wildlife Service, contains more than 7000 abstracts of reports of benefits provided by specific wetland areas (William Wilen,

US Fish and Wildlife Service, personal communication, 1987). But most of these efforts have not, on the whole, produced very useful results. Efforts to estimate the economic value of the biological productivity along with certain other natural functions that wetlands can provide, have resulted in estimates exceeding a hundred thousand US dollars per acre (Gosselink et al., 1974). These estimates, however, have little validity according to traditional economic thought. Usually, they are not estimates of the value of the functions that the wetland actually provides, but estimates of their capacity to provide certain functions, if called for. These estimates also typically use inappropriate prices for valuing the functions, and neglect the costs which would be associated with providing the services, if they were called for.

Other efforts, using more traditional economic approaches, have had limited success as well (Allen and Stevens, 1983). One example of an evaluation study which has enjoyed some acceptability was carried out by the US Army Corps of Engineers. This study calculated that the loss of all 8422 acres of wetlands within the Charles River Basin, Massachusetts, would lead to an increase in average annual flood damages of over US$17 million (Office of Technology Assessment, 1984). This study also emphasized the importance of the context, or geographic setting, for a particular wetland in determining the type and magnitude of the benefits it provides.

For example, wetlands located upstream of the city of Boston, or even relatively small areas located near flood-prone residential or farm communities, may offer greater flood-protection benefits than larger wetlands of the same type, but not located near developed land. Similarly, the actual benefits provided by a wetland area with high waterfowl habitat potential depend in part upon the location of the area, the scarcity of that type of environment within the region, and the existence, or potential existence, of wildlife in the area to make use of the habitat. Finally, the actual realization of benefits will depend, in part, upon the social significance of wetland environments within a community or region. Thus, for example, a community which values wildlife highly will benefit from its local wetlands in a way that a community with less interest in its wildlife resources does not.

Thus, it remains difficult, both conceptually and in practice, to quantify accurately the full range of benefits provided by the nation's wetlands, or even by specific wetland areas. A key factor affecting the need for wetland management, however, is the realization that, whatever the magnitude of these benefits, most of them do not accrue to the wetland owner. Instead, they are usually experienced by individuals living downstream of the wetland (as in the case of water quality improvement or flood control), or in areas which may be remote from the wetland itself (as in the case of wildlife). This divergence between private benefits and social benefits is a major cause of the market failures which result in excessive wetlands destruction.

## Wetland losses

Very little information is available about the rate at which US wetlands are being lost, degraded or altered. A survey conducted by the US Fish and Wildlife Service indicated that, between the mid-1950s and the mid-1970s, losses averaged 460 000 acres annually – equivalent to a loss rate of approximately one-half per cent per year (US Fish and Wildlife Service, 1983). A subsequent analysis, which attempted to adjust these data to take account of changes that occurred in government policy during the 1970s, estimated that the rate had fallen to 250 000 acres per year (Office of Technology Assessment, 1984). However, this revised estimate is controversial. The US Government (US Fish and Wildlife Service) is now conducting an updated national survey, but until its results become available, the only reliable information more recent than for the mid-1970s is provided by local or regional studies. These studies indicate that high loss rates are continuing – at least in the regions studied.

Just as wetlands can provide a wide range of services, they can also be altered in many diverse ways, thereby losing their ability to provide these functions (table 2.2). They may be changed physically by filling, draining, excavating, or clearing. Such alterations may affect some functions, but not others. For instance, they may eliminate a wetland's utility in providing habitat for some species, but increase it for others. Many types of alteration may have little effect on a wetland's ability to provide protection from flooding. Excavation could even increase the wetland's ability to recharge groundwater.

**Table 2.2: Methods of altering wetlands**

---

**Physical**

*Filling*: adding any material to change the bottom level of a wetland or to replace the wetland with dry land.
*Draining*: removing water from a wetland by ditching, tilling, pumping, and so on.
*Excavating*: dredging and removing soil from a wetland.
*Diverting water away*: preventing the flow of water into a wetland by removing upstream water, lowering nearby lake levels, or lowering groundwater tables.
*Clearing*: removing vegetation by burning, digging, application of herbicide, scraping, mowing, or otherwise cutting.
*Flooding*: raising water levels, either behind dams, or by pumping or channelling water into a wetland.
*Diverting or withholding sediment*: trapping sediment, through construction of dams, channelization, or other types of projects; thereby inhibiting the regeneration of wetlands in natural areas of deposition, such as deltas.
*Shading*: placing pile-supported platforms or bridges over wetlands, causing vegetation to die.
*Conducting activities in adjacent areas*: disrupting the "normal" interactions between wetlands and adjacent land areas, or incidentally affecting wetlands through activities at adjoining sites.

**Chemical**

*Changing nutrient levels*: increasing or decreasing levels of nutrients within the local water and/or soil system, forcing changes in wetland plant community.
*Introducing toxics*: adding toxic compounds to a wetland either intentionally (for example herbicide treatment to reduce vegetation) or unintentionally, thereby adversely affecting wetland plants and animals.
*Changes in salinity*: increasing the salinity level in the water by discharging saline substances or excavating canals which allow saline intrusion.

**Biological**

*Grazing and trampling*: consumption or destruction of vegetation by either domestic or wild animals.
*Disrupting natural populations*: reducing populations of existing species, introducing exotic species, or otherwise disturbing resident organisms.

---

Even if there are no physical changes, a wetland may also be altered by chemical contamination or biological changes. Such alterations may have little effect on a wetland's physical appearance, but can seriously interfere with its ability to perform certain beneficial functions. This was dramatically illustrated by the case of the Kesterson National Wildlife

Refuge in the San Joaquin Valley, California where widespread waterfowl mortalities and deformities have been caused by high concentrations of selenium in the local irrigation return flows entering the refuge. A recent literature review indicated that the potential for agricultural chemicals, particularly aerially-applied insecticides, to enter prairie potholes and reduce the quality of these wetlands for wildlife, is very high (Grue et al., 1988).

**Table 2.3: Wetland losses in the conterminous United States by probable cause of loss (in 000s of acres)**

| | Lost to | Gained from | Net loss | % of all losses |
|---|---|---|---|---|
| **Freshwater Wetlands** | | | | |
| Agriculture | 11 720 | 899 | 10 821 | 79.9 |
| Urban use | 925 | 38 | 887 | 6.3 |
| Deep water | 621 | 305 | 316 | 4.2 |
| Other use | 618 | 1828 | (1210) | 4.2 |
| Open water | 579 | 450 | 129 | 3.9 |
| Unconsolidated shore | 188 | 65 | 123 | 1.3 |
| Other non–vegetated | 25 | 12 | 13 | 0.2 |
| Saltwater vegetated | 1 | 25 | (24) | 0 |
| *Subtotal* (freshwater) | 14 677 | 3622 | 11 055 | 100.0 |
| **Saltwater wetlands** | | | | |
| Agriculture | 9 | 2 | 7 | 1.9 |
| Urban use | 107 | – | 107 | 22.2 |
| Deep water | 268 | 54 | 214 | 55.5 |
| Other use | 11 | 8 | 3 | 2.3 |
| Open water | – | – | – | – |
| Unconsolidated shore | 50 | – | 50 | 10.4 |
| Other non-vegetated | 12 | 44 | (32) | 2.5 |
| Freshwater vegetated | 25 | 1 | 24 | 5.2 |
| *Subtotal* (saltwater) | 482 | 109 | 373 | 100.0 |
| Total (all types) | 15 159 | 3731 | 11 428 | |

Source: Office of Technology Assessment (1984)

Wetland losses can be characterized in several different ways. Some focus on the type of resource lost. Others focus more on the type of alteration, or on the "causes" of the alterations. For example, the US Fish and Wildlife Service analyses focus primarily on the *characteristics* of the wetlands being lost. Their statistics (table 2.1) indicate that the largest losses between the mid-1950s and the mid-1970s, both in terms of absolute amounts and percentages of area lost, occurred in the "palustrine forested" and "emergent vegetation" categories. Their data also indicate that substantial areas were converted from "vegetated" to "non-vegetated" status during this period. This latter observation suggests that real losses were somewhat more serious than the total statistics indicate, at least in terms of the ability of the remaining wetlands to provide wildlife habitat. If non-vegetated wetlands are excluded, total losses amount to over 11 million acres (rather than 8.8 million acres), and the loss rate increases to 11 per cent. The gain in lacustrine wetlands reflects the construction of impoundments that occurred during the period, many of which flooded vegetated palustrine wetland areas.

The Office of Technology Assessment reprocessed these survey results to present the information in terms of the *way in which the land was being used after conversion* occurred. Their tabulation indicates that 80 per cent of the total wetlands lost were converted to agricultural uses. Agricultural conversions were, of course, particularly important for freshwater wetlands. In these areas, agriculture accounted for almost ninety-eight per cent of net wetland losses. Urban development, along with dredging and other forms of conversion to deep water habitat, were the most important causes of loss for coastal wetlands.

Another way of analysing the changes would be in terms of the *type of alteration* that occurred in terms of the different threats listed in table 2.3. Although it would be very difficult to collect nationwide data distinguishing each of the individual causes, it should be possible to distinguish between conversions resulting from the removal of water (by drainage, dyking, groundwater overdraft, and so on); those resulting from filling (primarily from the placement of fill material, but also from sedimentation); and those resulting from other physical, chemical or biological changes. This analysis has not been done. Any of this type of information which does exist usually demonstrates the various types of *physical* changes involved. Most *chemical* and *biological* changes are not included in loss estimates, unless they are accompanied by physical changes, because these are not likely to be identified by the aerial survey techniques usually used by the Fish and Wildlife Service. Thus, actual loss rates are probably significantly higher than those reported.

Another way of looking at losses is to distinguish between those that result from activities where conversion of the wetland was expected; those where the conversion is largely inadvertent; and those that result from "natural" changes. Most of the "management" concern is understandably focused on intended conversions – such as draining wetlands for agricultural production, or filling them for residential and commercial development. But large amounts of wetlands are also being converted inadvertently. Probably the most dramatic example is the Louisiana Coast, where an estimated forty to sixty square miles of wetlands a year are disappearing. Many of these coastal lands are formed by unconsolidated sediments deposited by the Mississippi River. Because this material consolidates slowly, the area depends on annual sediment deposits to keep it above sea level. But the construction of flood control levees along the mainstream of the river has cut off many these deposits, leaving the wetlands to sink slowly into the Gulf of Mexico, and disappear. Another cause of this disappearance is the construction of canals to allow drilling barges to explore the wetland areas for oil and gas deposits. These canals allow saltwater to enter the freshwater wetland areas, killing the local vegetation. They also speed up natural erosion and drainage processes.

In neither case are the economic activities – for example flood control or digging canals – undertaken for the purpose of destroying the wetlands, but this is the inadvertent result. Other examples of inadvertent conversion include chemical contamination from industrial plants or waste sites, non-point source pollution, sedimentation from upland erosion, and the elimination of water supplies through excessive groundwater pumping, or surface water diversions.

Some of these inadvertent conversions result from discrete, present-day activities. But many, such as the sinking of the Louisiana coastal wetlands, are the result of incremental decisions made in the past. Where this is the case, the conversion of wetlands would likely continue even if all new wetland converting activities were stopped entirely. Conceptually, a "base rate of conversion" exists, whose reduction will require more than just the cessation of new conversion activities.

Wetland conversions may also result from natural causes. Examples might include biological alterations, such as natural successional changes, or from physical and biological changes combined, such as natural changes in rainfall. Probably the most dramatic "naturally caused" conversion is that threatened by the rising sea levels which may accompany global climate change. Even in this case – as with many other "natural" conversions – human activities play a significant part in amplifying the natural changes.

A final way to look at wetland losses would be to estimate the *loss of functions* that the wetlands provide, rather than the physical losses. The "functional loss" may be greater or less than the gross physical losses. Draining a wetland, for instance, may diminish the amount of flood control benefits it provides, but would not eliminate them completely, even if the wetland were converted to another use that eliminated its habitat functions. Conversely, the habitat value of a wetland may be influenced by activities on the surrounding uplands. The development of these uplands may significantly diminish this habitat function, even though no apparent changes occur to the wetland itself. Unfortunately, readily applicable techniques for accurately measuring the functions provided by wetlands and their losses do not yet exist. Thus, there is no aggregate information about the value of these functions, much less about how they have changed over the years.

## Market failure

Most wetland conversions in the United States are, at least in major part, the result of market failure. In many cases, this market failure is accentuated by intervention failure.

Market failure is most evident in the case of "intended" conversions. In the United States, most of these conversions result from decisions by land owners that the private economic benefits of conversion will exceed the private conversion costs.

The private economic benefits of conversion are the increased income flows that will accrue to the owner after the wetlands are placed in some commercial use. In their natural state, wetlands will usually generate little monetary income. After conversion, they may be used to grow commercial crops, or for some other types of development. Draining wetlands may also reduce flooding on adjacent upland areas, and simplify the process of tilling and harvesting these lands.

Market failure can intrude on this process in any of several ways. For example, the land owners may inaccurately estimate the net benefits they themselves will realize from the conversion. There will also almost certainly be a difference between a land owner's private costs and benefits, and the economic benefits and costs accruing to society as a whole from the conversion. In calculating private benefits and costs, a land owner is likely to underestimate – because of a lack of knowledge – both the income that the wetlands can generate in their natural state, and the indirect benefits (such as groundwater recharge and flood control) that the wetlands naturally provide to the owner.

Although this type of failure can be significant, market failures resulting from a divergence between private and social benefits and costs are likely to be much more common, and much more costly in social terms. Most of the benefits provided by wetlands do not accrue to the wetland owner at all, but to other individuals. Thus, the wetland owner will generally only assess the direct costs of draining or filling the wetland, and will ignore most of the other beneficial functions that wetlands perform in their natural state. Other divergences between the private and social calculus may result from the social income after conversion being less than the private income, or the social costs of conversion being greater than the private costs. Many of these divergences are then exacerbated by intervention failure. The net result of the combination of all these factors, however, is that the *private* calculus of the net benefits from conversion is likely to appear to be much more favourable than the corresponding *public* calculus would be.

Market failure may also play a part in some "inadvertent" conversions. This could be the case when the individual deciding on the action that causes the conversion does not recognize that conversion is likely to result. This is a case of *information failure*. It is, of course, possible that the decision would not change even if this information were known, because the individual making the decision would not have had to pay the costs associated with these conversions in any event – they are external to his or her decision calculus. But this type of externality is an example of market failure.

This form of market failure, however, may not always result in excessive conversion. In many cases, the inadvertent conversion of wetlands results in financial benefits to the owner, and the individual causing the conversion is unable to capture these benefits.

The primary types of market failure in US wetlands, therefore, are lack of information about the costs associated with wetland conversions, and the fact that, in the case of private conversions (both intended and inadvertent), these costs are largely external to the individual who actually makes the decision. This leaves three primary cases in which market failure is *not* a serious problem:

(i) conversions in which the social benefits of conversion are greater than the social costs of conversion (elements of market failure may still exist in these cases, but their removal would not change the conversion decision);
(ii) inadvertent conversions that are solely the result of intervention failures; and,
(iii) "natural" conversions, that is, the result of ongoing ecologic processes.

## Intervention failure

Government interventions can affect the rate of wetland conversion in several different ways. In the United States, federal and state governments formally promoted the conversion of wetlands through financial incentives to individuals converting wetlands; through cost-sharing for wetland conversion activities; and through the construction of public projects to drain wetlands, or to protect them from being flooded. Whether such activities were actually examples of intervention failure is debatable. The purpose of the intervention was to convert wetlands, and they certainly succeeded in achieving that objective. However, these public policies were typically based on an incomplete understanding of the actual benefits and costs of wetland conversion. Thus, they may have been faulty policies, but they were not necessarily examples of intervention failure in the narrow sense. (Many of these policies have been changed over the past two decades, so that wetlands conversion is now rarely the primary purpose of government intervention activities.)

In fact, some efforts are now being made to undo the effects of these policies. For instance, the state of Florida has undertaken a major project to re-establish wetland areas along the Kissimmee River north of Lake Acachobee. The federal government drained these wetlands during the 1960s to create additional agricultural land. The state now recognizes that these wetlands provided substantial benefits (in the form of pollution control, wildlife habitat, and groundwater recharge), and is purchasing the lands back from the farmers, and building small dams in the channelized river in order to force it back into its original channel (The Conservation Foundation, 1989).

## *Types of impacts*

Intervention failures are still common, but they now result primarily from activities undertaken for some public purpose other than conversion itself. The impacts on the wetland may be an inseparable direct effect of the intervention activity, for instance when a wetland area is filled for the purpose of constructing a road. In most cases, however, the impacts on wetlands are more indirect. The linkage may be technical – for instance where the construction of a highway intercepts the flow of water that formerly supplied a wetland area. But probably the most significant indirect effects result from the way in which the government activity changes the apparent profitability of wetlands conversion to the private land owner. In these cases, the government action serves to accentuate a market failure situation that already exists.

*Direct impacts* A common cause of direct impacts is infrastructure investment, such as the construction of roads and dams. In some of these programmes, the government agency implementing the programme is the only party involved. For instance, the US Army Corps of Engineers (Corps) may construct a dam that floods a wetland area, or build a flood control project that drains one. In other instances, the government agency may only provide funding to an intermediary – often a different level of government – which actually undertakes the activity. For instance, the Federal Highway Administration (FHwA) provides funds to state governments for the construction of highways, and the US Environmental Protection Agency (EPA) provides funds to local governments for the construction of sewage treatment plants.

Not all direct impacts result from such construction activities, however. Some can occur as the result of government agencies such as the Bureau of Land Management (BLM) or the Department of Defense (DOD) routinely managing their extensive land holdings. Activities such as grazing cattle on public forest or range land can, for instance, alter existing wetlands, if insufficient regard is given to protecting wetland or riparian areas.

*Indirect impacts* Indirect impacts can occur when the government creates economic incentives which encourage private individuals to take actions that alter wetlands – or to *not* take actions which would protect them). For instance, agricultural price supports provide an incentive for farmers to cultivate additional acreage, possibly altering wetlands in the process. Special tax breaks can encourage various forms of economic development, some of which affect wetland areas. In practical terms, it is very difficult to predict (or to measure) how significant these indirect effects will be, and where they will occur.

This problem is further complicated by the fact that an individual policy may have both direct and indirect impacts. Thus, a highway built through a wetland has an obvious direct impact. But, even if the highway does not itself traverse the wetland, it may stimulate private residential and commercial development which does occur in wetlands – an indirect effect.

## *Types of government programmes which have resulted in intervention failure*

In the United States, the most significant government programmes resulting in intervention failure have been those relating to water resources development; to agricultural subsidies; to the construction of highways and other types of infrastructure; and to the management of public lands.

*Water resource programmes* A study by the Environmental Law Institute (1985) concluded that water resources projects have probably been the most important federal activity directly affecting wetlands over the years. Dam construction, navigation projects, irrigation projects, harbour dredging, stream channelization, impoundments for flood control, and coastal erosion control projects have all resulted in wetlands alteration, either directly or indirectly.

Wetland losses caused by the development of levees, navigation projects, and other federal water resource management projects have been significant in the lower Mississippi Valley's bottomland hardwood forest areas. This region contains substantial areas of valuable wetlands, which are experiencing continuing and rapid rates of conversion. At the time of European colonization, this area is thought to have included nearly 24 million acres of bottomland hardwood forested wetlands (Stavins, 1987). By 1937, only 11.8 million acres remained. Since that time, another 6.5 million acres have been cleared, mainly for agricultural development, leaving less than 5.2 million acres of wetlands today – about 20 per cent of the original acreage.

One study of this area (Stavins, 1987) concluded that flood protection was responsible for almost half of the conversion that had been experienced between 1935 and 1984. Rising agricultural prices and dry weather were also significant, but ultimately responsible for much less of the total conversion than flood protection and levee construction.

Coastal Louisiana is also experiencing significant wetland losses, again largely resulting from government intervention failures. Coastal Louisiana includes about 2.5 million acres of fresh to saline marshes, and 637 400 acres of forested wetlands dominated by bald cypress-tupelo swamps (Michot, 1984). This area accounts for about 40 per cent of the total acreage of coastal wetlands within the contiguous United States (Alexander et al., 1986). Although there are no published estimates of the original extent of Louisiana coastal wetlands, regional mapping studies (Gagliano et al., 1981; Gosselink et al., 1979) suggest that as much as 900 000 acres have been lost since 1900. The rate of loss has accelerated in recent years, and is now estimated to be about 40–60 square miles per year, or nearly 100 acres per day (Louisiana Wetland Protection Panel, 1987).

Although the loss of Louisiana's coastal wetlands is in part due to natural processes, for example sea-level rise and subsidence, the construction of an extensive system of federally-funded flood control, navigation, and hurricane-protection projects, as well as the private construction of canals – particularly for oil and gas exploration – have also been key sources of the problem (Louisiana Wetlands Protection Panel, 1987).

The Mississippi River and Tributaries (MR&T) Project evolved from the federal government's first authorized flood control effort (initiated in 1879). Of particular relevance to coastal Louisiana was the construction of about 449 miles of levees and river control structures within the Atchafalaya Basin Floodway. These modifications have interfered with natural overbank flooding that once transported freshwater and sediments into adjacent wetlands. The regulation of Atchafalaya River discharge to prevent the Mississippi River from changing its course has interfered with the large-scale "switching" process associated with delta building. Land building is now limited to a few deltaic areas, with much of the sediment that reaches the mouth of the river being channelled directly to deep water areas.

Major navigation channels have included the Gulf Intracoastal Waterway, a 302-mile-long channel initially constructed in 1938 and then enlarged in 1942; the Houma Navigation Canal; the Mississippi River-Gulf Outlet; Barataria Bay Waterway and Bayou-Segnette Waterway; and the Atchafalaya River Channel. These federally-supported projects involved the loss of thousands of acres of wetlands through the excavation and deposition of spoil materials. They also provided greater access to coastal Louisiana's oil and gas resources, inducing private development of vast networks of drainage and navigation canals. The canals have altered inland wetlands by changing flows and salinity patterns. They are also are considered a major direct cause of Louisiana's current land loss problems (Turner et al., 1982).

Hurricane protection projects, most of which were initiated during the 1960s, include the Lake Pontchartrain and Vicinity Hurricane Protection Project; the New Orleans to Venice Hurricane Protection Project; and the Larose to Golden Meadow Hurricane Protection Project. These projects, which are based on levee systems, have caused the loss of wetlands due to construction, excavation and drainage. In addition, those wetlands which survived within the protected areas are now subjected to increased development pressures.

In the arid regions of the western United States, irrigation, drainage, and water supply projects have significantly affected many wetland and riparian areas. The 400-mile-long Central Valley of California provides an example of the types of problems that are commonly experienced. At the time of European colonization, the Central Valley contained about four million acres of permanent, seasonal, and tidal wetlands including freshwater and brackish marshes and riparian wetlands (Dennis et al., 1984).

The Central Valley is now a premier agricultural area, accounting for billions of dollars in production. In the development process, it lost an estimated 90 per cent of its wetlands. Of the 373 584 acres remaining, 81 184 acres are publicly-owned and 292 400 acres are held privately. Agricultural development has been, and continues to be, the major direct cause of wetland losses in the area. Much of this development would have been impossible without federal and state supported irrigation, drainage and water supply projects.

As in the case of coastal Louisiana, the history of government water projects in the Central Valley is long and intricate. In 1850, just after California became a state, Congress initiated its first programme affecting wetlands in the valley, offering incentives for the construction of drains and levees. Both federal and state involvement in flood control and irrigation increased through the 1900s, with governments making a major commitment to the Central Valley Project (CVP) during the Great Depression.

Both the (federal) Central Valley Project and the (state) Water Project involved major hydrological modifications of an area ranging from north of San Francisco down to Los Angeles. These projects transport fresh water from the northern areas around San Francisco Bay, southward into the San Joaquin Valley. Today, the Central Valley Project consists of 20 dams and reservoirs, 8 electric generating facilities, 1437 miles of canals, and many miles of associated pipelines, aqueducts and drains (US Fish and Wildlife Service, 1987), and plans exist for more additions to the system.

These projects have caused the direct loss of many acres of wetlands, through construction activities, diversion of water, and interruption of seasonal flooding patterns. In addition, the ready availability of subsidized irrigation water has certainly stimulated increased agricultural development in the Valley, much of which occurred through the extensive conversion of privately-owned wetland areas.

Not only have these irrigation projects physically converted vast wetland areas, they threaten the chemical integrity of those that remain. In the early 1980s, irrigation return flows from a federal irrigation district were found to be seriously contaminating wetlands in the Valley's Kesterson Wildlife Refuge. This water picked up high levels of selenium, boron, and other contaminants from the land it was used to irrigate. The contamination then caused serious reproductive problems for waterfowl using the refuge. As a result, the refuge has been closed, and the government is now removing and burying all of the contaminated soil and vegetation. Ongoing research is also bringing to light similar problems in other areas in the San Joaquin Valley, as well as in other western US refuges and wetland areas.

Other water resource activities having significant impacts on wetlands include small watershed impoundments built to assist farmers (particularly important in the south and east); the licensing of hydroelectric facilities; the construction of waste water treatment facilities; and the allocation of water supplies.

The Department of Agriculture has itself undertaken or provided financial support for the construction of thousands of farm ponds and other small watershed projects. The farm ponds have drowned many small wetland areas, but have also increased others. The drainage programmes have only caused their conversion. Although these programmes are thought to have been significant in aggregate, a study of drainage decisions of "prairie potholes" in the north–central region of the United States concluded that drainage subsidies provided by the US government were probably significantly less important in drainage decisions than other factors (DOI, 1988). In part, this is because the cost of drainage in this part of the country is already relatively low.

The federal government licenses all hydroelectric facilities, as well as any other structures constructed in, or adjacent to, navigable waters. Most of the hydroelectric facilities currently being licensed are relatively small, but they can flood small wetland areas and disrupt water supplies to those which lie downstream. Licensing decisions, however, are required to take account of the impact of the proposed facility on wetlands.

The construction of waste water treatment facilities can affect wetlands directly, by locating sewers and treatment plants in wetland areas, and by stimulating residential and other developments in areas that would not otherwise have had access to this service. Because these facilities usually operate by gravity, they are most likely to be located in low-lying areas where wetlands are also concentrated.

In the western United States, state governments control the use and allocation of water supplies. Decisions allowing an applicant to divert water from a stream or withdraw it from the ground may deplete the supply of water to downstream wetlands. Such potential effects are rarely given consideration because most states do not recognize the use of water to sustain wetlands as a beneficial use of water.

*Other public works programmes* Next to water resource projects, highway construction is the type of public investment that has probably had the most significant impact on wetlands (Environmental Law Institute, 1985). Not only may the highways be constructed on fills placed in wetlands, but the highway embankment can also interfere with natural drainage patterns, cutting off water supplies to downslope wetlands. Highways, many of which are supported under the Federal Aid Highway Program (FAHP), were identified as significant factors affecting wetland conversions in the Prairie Pothole Region. A recent study of prairie pothole conversions found that highway drainage ditches are often used to drain adjacent wetlands (DOI, 1988). Although such use of the drainage ditches is illegal, effective enforcement has been lacking.

Finally, the use of salt to control ice on northern highways, along with pollutant run-off from roads and drainage ditches, can chemically alter downstream wetlands. Highways can also have significant indirect effects on wetlands. By providing better access to nearby lands, they can significantly increase their overall attractiveness for development.

Public transportation projects such as airports, railways, and metros can have similar direct and indirect effects, although airports are probably the most important of these in the United States. Wetland areas are often particularly attractive for airport developments because they are sometimes the only large areas undeveloped near urban centres. Other types of public investment that can have negative effects on the wetlands include electrical generating plant and transmission lines; public buildings; and parks. However, the cumulative impact of such investments has not been extensively studied, and is unlikely to be significant in the aggregate.

*Public land management* About one-third of US lands are owned and managed by the federal government, with another seven per cent being owned/managed by state and local governments. Within these public lands, which are concentrated in the western USA and Alaska, management policies and practices have important implications for wetlands. Western riparian wetlands have been altered by grants of transmission line rights-of-way, timber operations, public land grazing permits, and projects relating to recreational, or energy and mineral resource development on public lands. The use of public lands for grazing or harvesting timber have probably had the largest impacts, because of the amount of area devoted to these activities. However, no estimates are available regarding the magnitude of these activities on the conversion of publicly-owned wetlands.

*Economic benefit programmes* Governments undertake a wide range of programmes that provide economic benefits to the public at large, or to segments of the public. The economic benefits of some of these programmes sometimes create conditions that act as incentives, inducing the beneficiaries of the programmes to alter wetlands. Although the impact of these programmes on wetlands may be indirect, the extent of resulting wetlands alterations can be substantial.

Programmes to support agricultural prices and incomes are undoubtedly the most important of these. Two recent studies have attempted to quantify the amount of influence that these programmes have had in the past (DOI, 1988). One is a study of the Prairie Pothole Region in the north–central part of the country. The second is an analysis of the influence of various factors, including price supports, on agricultural incomes in the Mississippi Delta Region.

The Prairie Pothole Region comprises an area of about two hundred and twenty seven square miles. Most of the region is in Canada, but about sixty thousand square miles are located in the north–central portion of the United States (within the states of Montana, North Dakota, South Dakota, Iowa, and Minnesota). The region gets its name from its numerous small, shallow, scattered depressions of freshwater wetlands, and is a prime waterfowl production area in the central flyway (Tiner, 1984). Only seven million acres of the estimated original area of approximately twenty million acres of prairie wetlands in the USA remain, with losses continuing at an estimated rate of 20 000–33 000 acres annually.

Several studies conducted by (or for) the US Department of the Interior examined the effects of federal highway, water resource development, agriculture, and tax programmes on the wetlands of the Prairie Pothole Region. One study used a farm level stochastic economic simulation model to estimate the effects of various programmes on the net present values of six model farms representing the different sizes and types of farms, and the different agricultural conditions in the region (McColloch et al., 1987).

Using a ten-year simulation period (1975–84), the study examined the effect on the net present value of representative farms of programmes that might induce wetland conversions (such as cost-sharing for drainage; price and income supports; disaster assistance/crop insurance; interest rate subsidies; and favourable treatment of drainage costs for income tax purposes) as well as programmes established to protect wetlands (such as conservation easements). The results indicated that, regardless of what programmes were (or were not) in existence, net present values for all farm types were higher when wetlands were drained. Thus, drainage improved a farm's income, whether or not a particular federal programme was in place, although federal agriculture and tax programmes did make these conversions more profitable. Of all the factors examined, price and income supports had the greatest effect on the incentive to convert wetlands. Because the cost of drainage can be expected to increase over time as the least expensive drainage opportunities are exhausted, the relative importance of these incentives for total profitability may increase in the future.

A similar farm level simulation model was developed for the Mississippi Delta region to check the results of the econometric model discussed above (DOI, 1988). This analysis concluded that, in spite of the significant amount of conversion that has occurred in this region over the past two decades, under

1975–84 conditions, the conversion of bottomland hardwoods to agriculture was only marginally profitable, regardless of the existence of federal benefit programmes. The analysis did conclude, however, that federal agricultural and price support subsidies had increased the overall profitability of conversion.

Price supports are not the only agricultural programmes that may provide inducements for converting wetlands. For instance, the acreage-limitation provisions of the crop price programmes provides such incentives because they require farmers to "set aside" a certain *percentage* of the land that they have planted in the programme crop during the past few years. Thus they have an incentive to make this "base acreage" as large as possible in order to maintain as much production as they can in years when acreage limitations are in effect. This incentive may be significant enough to induce them to drain and plant wetlands in the programme crop even though this would not appear to be profitable when considering the income that these areas alone are likely to produce. The profit comes when they can include these areas in their "set-asides", and, therefore, grow crops on other more productive land elsewhere.

Other agricultural programmes that might induce wetland conversions include crop insurance programmes (which reduce the riskiness of farming); cost-sharing and technical assistance programmes; interest rate subsidies; and provisions of the income tax code. In particular, income tax provisions provide several types of incentives. One example is that the cost of conversion can be "expensed", that is, completely deducted from current income at the time the expenditures are made, rather than being treated as a capital investment that would have to be depreciated over a period of years. These codes have also sometimes treated the profits resulting from selling converted wetlands as capital gains which are usually taxed at lower tax rates than normal income. The tax codes may also encourage farmers to "overcapitalize" their enterprise. If so, this may lead to the conversion of wetlands for two reasons. One is that the wetlands become more of a nuisance when the farmer is using larger machinery, because it is more difficult to manoeuvre the machinery around them. The second is that the larger machinery makes it easier for the farmer to undertake additional conversions himself during the off-season.

The farm simulation studies undertaken for The Department

of the Interior attempted to analyse the degree of economic incentive that these programmes provided (DOI, 1988). In all cases, the studies found that the incentives were probably much less than those provided by the price supports themselves. However, several of these incentives may depend as much on psychological as on economic motivation, and the simulation studies were unable to estimate the strength of these psychological inducements.

Similar types of incentives may be provided to other, non-agricultural, segments of society. For example, some programmes provide low-interest loans for the construction of new industrial facilities or low-cost housing. Subsidized flood insurance (provided under the National Flood Insurance Program) probably stimulates the conversion of wetlands by promoting development in areas subject to flooding in many coastal and riverain areas. And the same types of income tax incentives that benefit farmers also apply to other land users. The effects of such programmes in sectors other than agriculture have not been studied in any detail. However, although they probably provide some economic incentive for wetland conversions, with the possible exception of the flood insurance programme, their net impact is likely to be small. Most of them would probably make only marginal differences in the basic economics of the conversion decision.

*Land use controls* Finally, land use controls, usually the responsibility of local governments, can encourage the conversion of wetlands in several ways. One is by zoning wetland areas for industrial or commercial developments. Large-lot zoning for residential areas may also result in development sprawling over a larger area than would otherwise occur, with resulting adverse impacts on wetlands. And rising property tax obligations can create an incentive to develop land that would otherwise be kept as open space/wetlands.

## Remedial measures

The United States has adopted several different types of remedial measures that attempt to address both market and intervention failures affecting wetlands. Most of these remedies were implemented after the most recent survey of the nation's wetlands resources was completed in the late 1970s. For this reason, no empirical data exists to illustrate how successful they have been. Some observers think that they have had a significant effect on slowing down the rate of wetlands conversion, but, as indicated above, recent research suggests that wetland loss rates in the USA remain high.

## *Market failures*

Both regulatory and non-regulatory programmes have been adopted at the federal and state levels to address the problem of market failure.

*Regulatory programmes* Wetland conversions can be regulated by any one of three types of programme. Only one of these types is primarily concerned with the wetland itself. The other two have some other primary regulatory focus, but may also protect wetlands indirectly in the process of achieving their primary goal.

The type of regulatory programme focusing on the wetlands themselves generally limits or prohibits certain types of alterations to the resource. For instance, it can be made illegal to drain or place fill in a wetland, even though it is privately owned, without receiving prior permission from the regulatory agency.

A second type of regulatory programme attempts to control certain activities that may alter wetlands. For instance, regulations that require a hydroelectric facility to obtain a government licence before it can be built may prohibit the responsible agency from issuing the licence when significant conversion of wetlands would result. A third type of regulatory programme focuses on the functional values of wetlands, particularly on their importance as habitat for certain wildlife species. These programmes can limit proposed alterations, if they would significantly interfere with these values.

At the federal level, the only example of the first type of programme is section 404 of the Clean Water Act. This section of the law requires anyone intending to place dredged or fill material in the waters of the United States to obtain a permit. Most wetlands are included in the definition of "waters of the United States", although the definition and delineation of protected areas has often been controversial. The law does not explicitly control other types of alteration, such as drainage. However, if the drainage process involves the placement of material in the wetland – for instance, while excavating a drainage ditch – a permit is required.

Detailed regulations and guidelines have been promulgated to govern the implementation of the Clean Water Act. They are intended to discourage alterations, if the purpose for which the alteration is proposed is not dependent on having access to water; and to minimize the extent of alteration, if the proposed activity is allowed to proceed. The permittee may also be required to provide compensation for any wetlands that are converted. The Environmental Protection Agency can also set aside particular wetlands that are important in terms of certain specified functions they provide.

Some states have similar regulatory programmes which are often more extensive in terms of the types of alterations they control than the section-404 programme itself. Most coastal states also have planning programmes which serve to discourage wetlands alterations in coastal regions. Local governments, which are usually responsible for zoning and other land-use-development controls, may also designate wetland areas for purposes other than development.

Undoubtedly, these programmes have been successful in reducing the amount of wetlands filled or otherwise converted for development purposes. However, there are no "hard" estimates of *how* successful they have been. Under the section-404 programme, the Corps receives approximately twelve thousand permit applications annually. An indeterminate amount of wetland is also converted illegally, or under the conditions of "general permits", which allow small areas to be filled without obtaining a specific permit. The section-404 programmes have been aimed primarily at restricting large new development proposals, and are, therefore, unlikely to affect more than 10–15 per cent of total wetland conversions in the United States.

The second type of regulatory programme – regulations covering activities that may alter wetlands indirectly – includes the many rules that require different types of facilities to obtain permits from federal or state agencies before they can be built, or before they can begin operation. These include hydroelectric facilities; other types of electrical generating facilities; electric transmission lines; oil and gas pipelines; mines; bridges; and new industrial facilities, for example for discharge or emissions permits. As a result of various laws and executive orders, the responsible federal and state agency usually can (and often must) consider the impacts of these facilities on wetlands, when evaluating the original application for a development permit.

Programmes regulating water pollution and waste disposal may also serve to protect wetlands from certain types of alteration. Water pollution laws can protect wetlands from chemical contamination by waste water discharges. However, very little consideration has been given to the question of whether special water quality standards should be established for wetlands in recognition of such facts as: (a) they tend to accumulate certain types of pollutants; and (b) some of their functions, such as wildlife habitat, may be particularly sensitive to chemical contamination. Another type of water pollution control programme that may protect wetlands is directed at controlling non-point sources of pollution. These programmes may protect wetlands from contamination by pesticides and other toxic substances carried off the land by stormwater, as well as from sedimentation, which can eventually fill in the wetland area.

Solid waste disposal laws protect wetlands by prohibiting the disposal of solid and hazardous wastes in wetland areas; by requiring the removal of hazardous wastes which have previously been disposed of in such areas; and by controlling leakage from underground storage tanks, which could contaminate wetland areas.

The only examples of the third type of regulatory approach are those programmes established to protect endangered species and migratory wildlife. Under the Endangered Species Act, the conversion of wetlands may be prohibited if they provide habitat crucial to the survival of endangered species. The Migratory Bird Treaty can provide similar protection, if the alteration of wetland areas will result in the destruction of migratory wildlife protected under this Treaty. The Migratory Bird Treaty, for instance, provided the legal basis for the Department of the Interior to cut off irrigation water supplies to certain farmers in California's Central Valley, because the irrigation return flow from their lands was poisoning migratory waterfowl in that state.

*Non-regulatory programmes* A number of different "non-regulatory" programmes have been adopted by different levels of government in an attempt to protect wetlands. These programmes can be thought of as addressing the problem of market failure. They include:

(i) public education about the benefits that wetlands provide;
(ii) tax incentives for individuals who protect wetlands;
(iii) subsidies for individuals protecting wetlands; and
(iv) public acquisition of wetland areas.

Public education programmes are aimed at correcting the market failures resulting from incomplete or inaccurate information. Such programmes are typically carried out by federal, state, and local agencies, as well as by a number of private, non-profit organizations. The education efforts focus on the values that wetlands provide; on the importance of protecting these areas; and on the various programmes which exist for this purpose.

In some areas, government agencies have also undertaken wetland protection plans, which identify those wetland areas considered to be the most valuable. Such plans can alert land developers to the existence and importance of these sites, and thereby discourage their conversion. The Fish and Wildlife Service, often in association with state agencies, is also undertaking a long-term project to map all the wetlands in the United States. Although these maps do not indicate the relative importance of the wetlands they identify, they do provide information for developers and land owners to help them avoid altering wetland areas.

Government tax incentive and subsidy programmes attempt to correct market failures by providing the land owner with some financial reward for preserving wetlands, in order that they can continue to provide their "public" values. For example, the federal (and many state) income tax laws allow land owners who donate their wetlands, or who provide conservation easements on these lands, to qualified non-profit organizations, to deduct the value of the donations as charitable gifts. Some states and localities also allow open space such as wetlands to be assessed at low values when computing property tax liabilities.

The federal government has also implemented several programmes that provide payments to individuals to protect wetlands. The largest of these programmes is the "conservation reserve" programme implemented by the Food Security Act of 1986. This programme pays farmers an annual rental for keeping certain lands out of production for a ten-year period. Although the programme is primarily directed at highly erodible lands, it may include former wetlands if they are subject to wind erosion, or if they serve as buffer strips along streams or other waterways. The government will also share in the costs of converting these lands from crops to natural cover, including wetlands.

The federal "water bank" programme pays farmers, primarily in certain important waterfowl production states, to preserve wetlands that they own. The agreements usually run for a period of ten years, but many are then renewed. Several states also have similar subsidy programmes that supplement those provided by the federal government.

Finally, various government and private non-profit organizations acquire wetlands expressly for the purpose of protecting them. These "acquisition" programmes often focus on the most valuable wetland areas for waterfowl production, and the acquisition is both politically and financially supported (directly or indirectly) by hunters. The acquisition can be in "fee simple" (that is, full ownership of the land) or it can involve only conservation easements. Several special funds have been established for such acquisition efforts, although these funds are sometimes used for acquiring any type of open space, not just wetlands.

Very few analyses have been conducted to determine the effectiveness of these "non-regulatory" programmes. The education programmes have undoubtedly been important, both in reducing the proclivity of land owners to drain wetlands, and in encouraging more aggressive public and private efforts to protect them. Tax incentives have undoubtedly encouraged charitable donations, although the significance of these incentives is probably limited, because wetlands tend to have low market values in the first place.

The farm simulation studies conducted for the Department of the Interior (DOI, 1988) attempted to assess the importance of the water bank programme and other subsidy programmes in encouraging farmers to preserve wetlands in the Prairie Pothole Region. The results indicated that these programmes do influence the relative profitability of conversion, in addition to reducing the financial risks faced by the farmer. However, in only one of the representative farms would the importance of the programmes be a key determinant in the decision of whether or not to convert. On the other hand, the importance of these programmes may be larger than the results of this study suggest. For one thing, there were several analytical problems encountered by the study itself. For another, farmers have consistently attempted to enroll more land in the banking programmes than available budgets would support. This implies that the banking programmes do play a significant role in farmers' decisions, at least in psychological terms.

### *Intervention failures*

In recent years, the federal government has adopted, through legislation, executive orders, and agency guidelines, a number of mechanisms for reducing inadvertent wetland impacts resulting from intervention failures. Some state governments have adopted similar protective measures, although these are usually less aggressive and fewer in number than federal initiatives. Local governments may also incorporate more sensitivity to wetlands in their land-use planning and control processes, and are very likely to be influenced by guidelines issued by the state or federal government when intergovernmental transfers are involved. The following analysis, however, focuses primarily on actions at the federal level.

The earliest federal law requiring agencies to assess the impact of their actions on wetlands was the National Environmental Policy Act (NEPA) with its "environmental impact statement" (EIS) requirement. If a proposed action is likely to cause significant environmental impacts, the resulting EIS offers a means to assess and mitigate wetland impacts. Federal agencies with jurisdiction and expertise, such as the EPA and the Fish and Wildlife Service, must both review and comment on EISs. The EPA can also raise concerns about federal projects to the Council on Environmental Quality in the Executive Office of the President. A majority of states have also adopted EIS requirements, or their functional equivalent.

The Fish and Wildlife Co-ordination Act also encourages federal agencies to consider the impacts of their projects on wetlands. Usually implemented in association with the NEPA requirements, the Act requires federal agencies to consider the impacts of their projects on fish and wildlife, and gives the Fish and Wildlife Service authority to review and comment on the wetland impacts of such projects. However, the Service's views are only advisory.

In 1977, President Carter gave increased emphasis to wetlands protection by issuing two executive orders, one pertaining to wetlands (EO 11990), and the second relating to floodplains (EO 11988). These executive orders were intended to reduce the costs of unnecessary wetland and floodplain development. Government agencies must also obtain section-404 permits when undertaking activities that would result in the placement of dredged or fill material in wetland areas.

As noted above, no assessment of the effectiveness of these various requirements has been conducted, and little effort has been devoted to monitoring federal agency compliance with them. Nevertheless, it does appear from the large number of references to wetlands, and to the relevant executive orders in environmental impact statements, that the requirements have at least made federal agencies much more aware of the need to avoid altering wetlands. A regional wetland study for the Office of Technology Assessment in North Carolina concluded that "the Soil Conservation Service dramatically changed their [*sic*] policies and procedures in wetland areas as a result of this directive and others such as the National Environmental Policy Act" (Office of Technology Assessment, 1984).

*Water resource projects* Several recent Congressional actions have sought to mitigate the adverse impacts of water-resources projects on wetlands and other environmental resources. Provisions in the Water Resources Development Act of 1986 increased the amount of local cost-sharing required for such projects, which should help to restrain both the number and size of new projects. The Act also requires fish and wildlife mitigation to occur before, or concurrently with, project construction. However, the degree to which mitigation will be undertaken will depend upon the total level of funding that Congress appropriates for this purpose.

In addition to these general provisions affecting new projects, the Act de-authorized several projects, in part because of their likely affect on wetlands, that had been authorized in previous years. Another Act dealt specifically with the Garrison

Diversion project which was projected to have a significant impact on wetlands in its service area. Congress reduced the affected acreage from 250 000 to 100 000 acres and, among other things, established a Federal/State Wetlands Trust to protect, enhance, restore, and manage prairie pothole wetlands (National Audubon Society, 1987).

*Swampbuster* In 1986, in an effort to reduce the number of wetland conversions being induced by agricultural price supports, Congress enacted a "swampbuster" provision in the Food Security Act (Title XII, PL 99-198). This provision makes persons cultivating crops on wetlands converted, for example drained or filled, after 23 December 1985 ineligible to receive any federal farm programme benefits. The swampbuster provision does not apply sanctions to the wetlands alteration itself, but only when the converted lands are planted with crops.

The penalty applies to all agricultural production under the control of the person who converted the land, not solely to the crops grown on the converted land. However, it only applies in those years when the converted land is actually planted in annual crops. Thus, even after converting the land, the farmer can avoid the penalty provisions in years when price supports and other agricultural programmes are likely to be important by not planting crops on the converted land. The provisions also do not apply if the converted land is planted in perennial crops, such as orchards or pasture. The law and its associated regulations also exempted lands for which the conversion process was initiated prior to December 1985, and adopted a rather loose definition of what constituted an "initiation" of the conversion process.

Although it is too early to assess the effectiveness of these provisions, several analyses have concluded that they are unlikely to stop the conversions of wetlands for agricultural purposes entirely, although they have a significant impact on the amount of conversion in some regions.

The farm simulation studies conducted for the Department of the Interior suggest that the swampbuster provisions can both reduce the income from, and increase the riskiness of, farming (DOI, 1988). Thus, they may discourage conversions in areas where the economics of conversion are already marginal, such as the Mississippi Delta region. However, in areas such as the Prairie Pothole Region, where conversion is clearly profitable, they may have a limited impact. These conclusions were similar to those reached in a 1988 study which analysed the likely effectiveness of these provisions on the basis of county data on conversion costs, production costs, and the extent to which farmers in the county receive agricultural programme benefits (Heimlich, 1988). This study estimated that, nationally, the penalties would discourage conversion on only about thirty-five per cent of the wetlands where conversion to agricultural purposes is considered likely. The influence, however, was much greater in some areas than others.

*Income tax provisions* The Tax Reform Act of 1986 (PL 99-514) removed several tax inducements to wetland conversions. One was to eliminate reduced tax rates for capital gains. Thus, the sale of land that has been "improved" by drainage is now taxed at the same rate as ordinary income. (Furthermore, the conversion of wetlands for agricultural purposes is explicitly prohibited from receiving treatment as capital gains, even if the "old" capital gains provisions should be reintroduced in the future. However, conversions for non-agricultural purposes are not so prohibited, and therefore could conceivably receive such benefits in the future.) A second change was to disallow the expensing of the costs of any land clearing or water diversion which results in wetland conversion. A third was to eliminate the 10 per cent investment tax credit, which had previously been used to offset costs of drainage tile or similar wetland-drainage engineering. The Act also eliminated some other tax provisions, such as rapid depreciation of buildings, which had favoured investments in real estate development over other investments. Thus, most of the incentives provided by the tax law are now gone. However, these changes are unlikely to make a significant impact on the total amount of conversion because these incentives were probably not crucial to the original conversion decision in many cases anyway.

## Conclusion

Over 50 per cent of the wetlands that existed in the conterminous United States at the time the first Europeans settled the country have since disappeared. Many of these losses were the result of intentional government activities which actively promoted the conversion of wetlands to agricultural and other purposes. Between the mid-1950s and the mid-1970s, the rate of wetland loss averaged close to half a million acres per year.

There is scant information available on what the current loss rate is, although available evidence indicates that it is still high. Both market failure and intervention failure are important causes of these losses. However, since the early 1970s the federal government and many state governments have instituted a number of regulatory and non-regulatory programmes for the purpose of reducing both types of failure. Little information exists on the success of these programmes. A recent review of wetlands policy, however, recommends a wide range of new initiatives in order to achieve a national goal of no-net-loss of the remaining wetlands (National Wetlands Policy Forum, 1988).

## References

Alexander, C. E., M. A. Broutman and D. W. Field, *An Inventory of Coastal Wetlands of the USA* (Washington DC: National Oceanic and Atmospheric Administration, US Department of Commerce, 1986).

Allen, P. G. and T. H. Stevens, *Use of Hedonic Price Technique to Evaluate Wetlands* (Amherst: Water Resources Research Center, University of Massachusetts, 1983).

Conservation Foundation, *Keeping Florida Afloat: a Case Study of Governmental Responses to Increasing Demands on a Finite Resource* (Washington DC: The Conservation Foundation, 1989).

Conservation Foundation, *Background Papers for the National Wetlands Policy Forum* (Washington DC: The Conservation Foundation, in press).

Dennis, N. B., M. L. Marcus and H. Hill, *Status and Trends of California Wetlands*. Report to the Assembly Committee on Natural Resources (Sacramento: State Capitol (CA), 1984).

Department of the Interior (DOI), *The Impact of Federal Programs on Wetlands, Vol. 1: The Lower Mississippi Alluvial Plain and the Prairie Pothole Region* (Washington DC: US Department of the Interior, 1988).

Environmental Law Institute, *Federal Policies which may Adversely Affect the Quantity and Quality of Wetlands*. Working Paper prepared for the US Environmental Protection Agency (Washington DC, 1985).

Gagliano, S. M., K. J. Meyer-Arendt and K. M. Wicker, "Land Loss in the Mississippi River Deltaic Plain", *Transactions, Gulf Coast Association of Geological Societies*, vol. 31, pp.295–300 (1981).

Gosselink, J. G., C. C. Cordes and J. W. Parsons, *An Ecological Characterization Study of the Chenier Plain Coastal Ecosystem of Louisiana and Texas* FWS/OBS-78/9-78/11 (3 vols) (Slidell (LA): Office of Biological Service, US Fish and Wildlife Service, 1979).

Gosselink, J. G., E. P. Odum and R. M. Pope, *The Value of the Tidal Marsh* (Baton Rouge: Louisiana State University Center for Wetland Resources (LSU-SG-74-03), 1974).

Grue, C. E., M. W. Time, G. A. Swanson, S. M. Borthwick and L. R. Deweese, *Agricultural Chemicals and the Quality of the Prairie Pothole Wetlands for Adult and Juvenile Waterfowl – What are the Concerns?* Paper presented at the National Symposium on Protection of Wetlands from Agricultural Impacts (Fort Collins: Colorado State University, 1988).

Hankla, D. L., *New Orleans to Venice, Louisiana, Hurricane Protection Project* (1984).

Heimlich, R. E., *The Swampbuster Provision: Implementation and Impact*. Paper presented at the National Symposium on Protection of Wetlands from Agricultural Impacts (Fort Collins: Colorado State University, 1988).

Kramer, R. and L. Shabman, "Incentives for Agricultural Development of US Wetlands: a Case Study of Bottomland Hardwoods of the Lower Mississippi River", in: *Resources for the Future: Agriculture and the Environment*. Annual Policy Review of the National Center for Food and Agricultural Policy (Washington DC, 1986).

Leitch, J. A. and W. C. Nelson, *Review of the Effect of Selected Federal Programs on Wetlands in the Prairie Pothole Region* (Minneapolis (MN): Barton-Aschman Associates Inc., 1986).

Louisiana Wetland Protection Panel, *Saving Louisiana's Coastal Wetlands: The Need for a Long-Term Plan of Action* (Washington DC: Louisiana Geological Survey and the US Environmental Protection Agency EPA-230-02-87-026, 1987).

McColloch, P. R., D. J. Wissman and J. Richardson, "An Assessment of the Impact of Federal Programs on Prairie Pothole Drainage", *National Wetlands Newsletter*, vol. 9, no. 4, pp.3–6 (1987).

Michot, T. C., *Louisiana Coastal Area Study: Interim Report on Land Loss and Marsh Creation*. Planning Aid Report submitted to New Orleans District US Army Corps of Engineers (New Orleans (LA), 1984).

National Audubon Society, *Audubon Wildlife Report* (San Diego (CA): Academic Press Inc., 1987).

National Wetlands Policy Forum, *Protecting America's Wetlands: an Action Agenda* (Washington DC: The Conservation Foundation, 1988).

Office of Technology Assessment, *Wetlands: their Use and Regulation* (Washington DC: US Congress, 1984).

Roe, R. A., "A New Direction in Water Resources Development", *Environmental Law Reporter 10144* (May, 1987).

Stavins, R., *Conversion of Forested Wetlands to Agricultural Uses: An Econometric Analysis of the Impact of Federal Programs on Wetland Depletion in the Lower Mississippi Alluvial Plain, 1935–1984* (New York (NY): Environmental Defense Fund, 1987).

Tiner, R. W., *Wetlands of the United States: Current Status and Recent Trends* (Newton Corner (MA): US Fish and Wildlife Service, 1984).

Turner, R. E., R. Costanza and W. Scaife, "Canals and Wetland Erosion Rates in Coastal Louisiana", in: Boesch, D. F. (ed.), *Proceedings of the Conference on Coastal Erosion and Wetland Modification in Louisiana: Causes, Consequences, and Options* (Washington DC: FWS/OBS-82/69, 1982).

US Fish and Wildlife Service, *Status and Trends of Wetlands and Deepwater Habitats in the Conterminous United States, 1950s to 1970s* (Washington DC: US Government Printing Office, 1983).

US Fish and Wildlife Service, *Fish and Wildlife Coordination Report* (Lafayette (LA)).

US Fish and Wildlife Service, *Federal Involvement in the Water Resources of the Central Valley* Draft Discussion Paper by Felix Smith (Sacramento (CA): 1987).

US Water Resources Council, *Options for Cost-Sharing, Part 5a: Implementation and OM&R Cost-Sharing for Federal and Federally Assisted Water and Related Land Programs*, p.41 (Washington DC, 1975).

Wahl, R., *Bureau of Reclamation Subsidies for Irrigation*. Draft paper (Washington DC: Office of Policy Analysis, US Department of the Interior, 1987).

Wilen, W., US Fish and Wildlife Service, personal communication (1987).

# 3

# UNITED KINGDOM

Kerry Turner

## The UK wetland environment: an overview

All of the UK's main wetland types – wet meadows (freshwater and saline marshes); estuarine wetlands and saltmarshes; upland blanket bog and lowland raised bog – have suffered considerable losses during the twentieth century, due to a combination of both market and intervention failures. It has been claimed that, in aggregate, the UK has been losing some 150 000 acres of wetlands a year, due solely to agricultural drainage and agricultural land-use intensification. This estimate was probably accurate until at least the 1970s and early 1980s on the mainland, and as recently as the late 1980s in Northern Ireland. Both wet meadows and saline coastal marshes, in particular, have suffered. Table 3.1 illustrates the scale of these losses for four important coastal grazing marsh areas since the 1930s.

The original fenlands of East Anglia – Cambridgeshire, Lincolnshire and Norfolk – represent an extreme example of the impact of land drainage. Today, less than one per cent of the original fens remain intact, after some three hundred years of intermittent drainage activity. Between the early 1950s and the 1980s, some fifteen per cent of the salt marshes in England and Wales (including 4000 ha of sites with special scientific interest) were lost to agricultural and/or industrial land-reclamation schemes. Some eighty-four per cent of Britain's raised bog had disappeared by 1978 because of afforestation, agricultural reclamation and commercial peat cutting. Currently, only about 1300 ha (60 per cent of the original stock) still contains vigorously growing sphagnum-dominated bog.

**Table 3.1 Loss of coastal grazing marsh in eastern England**

| Area | Period studied | Original wetland stock (ha) | Area remaining (ha) | Loss (%) |
|---|---|---|---|---|
| Broadland (Norfolk and Suffolk) | 1930–84 | 19 992 | 12 646 | 37 |
| East Essex | 1938–81 | 11 749 | 2083 | 82 |
| North Kent | 1935–82 | 14 750 | 7675 | 48 |
| Romney Marsh (Kent) | 1931–80 | 16 000(c.) | 7200 | 55 |

*Source*: Royal Society for the Protection of Birds (1987)

In Northern Ireland, only 27 000 ha of raised bog now remains from a once very extensive stock. Of the habitat that still survives, only about eight per cent is in an intact state, with an uncut surface. Blanket bog areas have been less affected by agricultural reclamation and peat-cutting, but they too have been much denuded, and are in any case extremely rare habitats to begin with. The total global blanket-bog resource is only about ten million ha, of which only one million ha is found in Britain. Afforestation schemes have also posed a major threat to the remaining areas of blanket bog.

Industrial and agricultural pollution (in some places combined with sewerage effluent) have also served, in subtle and complicated ways, to degrade wetland ecosystems. In the majority of cases, water-borne pollution has been the main problem, but some upland wetlands have also suffered degradation due to air pollution in the form of acid deposition. The degradation process usually results in a series of latent damage impacts, including the loss of species diversity.

Many scientists believe that the progressive, and even accelerating, global accumulation of atmospheric trace gases – carbon dioxide, methane, nitrous oxide and CFCs – will eventually induce a significant climate modification. One impact of this "greenhouse effect" may be a rise in mean sea-levels, possibly accompanied by an increased frequency of extreme storm events. UK saltmarshes, coastal marshes and intertidal mudflats, as well as other ecosystems, could be radically changed, or lost altogether, with these changes of sea-level parameters. Previous exploitation of peat wetlands has also, according to some scientists, contributed to the release of $CO_2$ to the atmosphere and, thus, to potential global warming.

## The importance of wetlands: functional and structural values

There is a growing awareness that those wetlands which remain relatively undegraded represent more socially valuable economic resources (social value = direct use value + indirect use value + non-use value) if they are left in their natural, semi-natural, or only slightly modified states. If such wetlands are radically altered and intensively managed, there is likely to be a net loss in social value.

UK wetlands, in aggregate, provide all of the following functions/services: flood storage; flood protection; important wildlife habitats; nutrient cycling/storage and related pollution control, landscape and amenity services; recreational services; non-use benefits (that is, existence and bequest value); agricultural output, other commercial output (for example, reeds); shoreline protection and storm-damage buffer zones; and extended food-web control.

Unfortunately, there are no systematic studies available on the monetary valuation of these wetland functions and services in the UK, although some fragmentary evidence does exist.

Saltmarshes and estuarine wetlands are highly productive ecosystems, which are intimately linked to the surrounding coastal waters. Their *functional services* provide *indirect-use* values. In many estuaries, there is a net outflow of materials to intertidal flats and coastal waters, sustaining a dense invertebrate fauna to feed wading birds and fish, especially during the critical larval stages. The North Sea coastal habitats, for example, are particularly rich in marine life. The largest whitefish port in the North Sea Basin, Peterhead in Scotland, serves some four hundred boats, and handles an annual catch with a dockside value of £75 million.

Another *functional service* provided by saltmarshes is their coastal zone buffering capacity. These marshes serve to dissipate some of the sea's wave energy as the water flows over the vegetation. It was estimated in 1981 that the building of sea walls, fronted by saltmarsh, on part of the eastern coast of England cost some £14 000 per kilometre. A wall not protected by saltmarsh requires much more reinforcement, and could cost up to £300 000 per kilometre, depending on local conditions. If "greenhouse-induced" sea-level and storm-frequency changes actually materialize, future coastal defence strategies will become significantly more expensive. If sea-level were to rise by a metre or more by the year 2050, the estimated capital cost of replacing UK sea defences, by conventional means, may be as much as £5000 million (1988 prices). Given the almost inevitable rise of at least some magnitude in sea-level, the use of combined – natural and engineered – defence strategies may well prove to be the most cost-effective option at a number of locations for responding to global warming.

Under natural conditions, UK peatlands – upland and lowland bogs and marshes – normally act as net carbon "sinks" (Armentano and Menges, 1986). Functionally, they are important links in the global cycling of carbon dioxide, and other atmospheric gases. Drainage of these peatlands and their exploitation via peat extraction have contributed to global shifts in the balance of carbon movement between wetlands and the atmosphere over the last two centuries. The result is that many wetlands are now net carbon *sources*, that is, they actually contribute to increased $CO_2$ releases to the atmosphere.

Grazing marshes – freshwater and saline – may also be providing a pollution-buffering function, although hard scientific evidence of this is not available for the UK. What can be said is that one typical component of UK marshes, reedbeds, are being tested as "natural" sewage-effluent treatment mechanisms, so far with quite encouraging results. High levels of nitrogen and phosphorus removal have been achieved in trial conditions. Cost estimates are not available for the UK, but West German data has indicated that a one hectare reedbed servicing the sewage output from a community of 2700 people, costs 25 per cent less than a conventional treatment plant.

Economies of scale, pollution loading, and treatment efficiencies remain to be precisely quantified. Another example of what has been called root-zone biotechnology effluent treatment, involves the fringing of some landfill waste disposal sites with reedbeds, in order to restrict leachate transference.

UK coastal wetlands have a distinctive *ecosystem structure* which also yields *direct use values*. These values include recreational value, aesthetic appreciation, scientific research, and education enhancement. Large and diverse resident and migratory bird populations, for example, are found along most of the UK coastline where wetlands occur. At present, UK estuaries are the wintering grounds for more than 50 per cent of Europe's waders. A number of important bird species nest in saltmarshes, including redshank; oyster catcher; lapwing; ringed plover; curlew; and dunlin. Gulls, terns, wildfowl; and some passerines are also represented. Among all these species, saltmarshes are generally regarded as being the most important for the redshank, since some 60 per cent of all UK redshank nest in the country's saltmarshes.

The continued loss of intertidal habitats would also pose a significant threat to migratory shorebird populations, which use these areas as wintering quarters. There is increasing evidence that competition between birds limits the numbers that can use a particular estuary, or a part of it. Evidence from several species of waders suggests that, through interference, a given abundance of food can only carry a certain density of birds, and, for some species, many estuaries are already at capacity (ITE, 1989).

UK estuaries lie in a key position on the East Atlantic Flyway. They support 20 per cent – or more than a million birds – of the total number of waders wintering on the Atlantic seaboard of Europe and Africa. They also provide crucial stopover sites for birds migrating between northern breeding areas and wintering areas in southern Europe and west Africa.

In terms of direct use value, UK grazing marshes – freshwater and saline – in their semi-natural state, support floristically-rich and diverse natural grasslands. Freshwater drainage (dyke) systems form a valuable habitat for aquatic plants, insects and amphibians, some of which are of national or international importance. The marshes in some of these areas are also important breeding grounds for wading birds, for example curlew, snipe and corncrake. Traditional practices, such as low-intensity grazing, reed cultivation, and controlled waterfowl hunting are largely compatible with the maintenance of the semi-natural wetland ecosystem structure. The marshes also provide a landscape and amenity resource much prized by conservationists, in addition to offering a wide range of recreational services.

The output of commercial reed, sedge and willow from wetlands is thought to be fairly substantial, but again, economic valuations are not readily available. The total market demand for reed (roof thatching) in the UK has been estimated to be approximately 36 000 tonnes, worth about £1.25 million (1988/89 prices). In the past, most domestic demand was met from British reedbeds. But since the late 1970s foreign reed has penetrated the UK market, and now accounts for some 28 000 tonnes. The rate of import-penetration has been accelerated because of a decline in UK reed quality, which results in premature thatch decay on roofs. The reasons for the loss of reed quality are not fully understood, but nutrient enrichment of wetlands may play a part, along with a more hostile (acidic) roof environment due to atmospheric pollution.

Wetlands also create *non-use value* (existence and bequest value) mainly because of their physical structure. This structure involves tangible items, such as plants and animals, along with the landscape itself, both of which the public is coming to recognize as nationally and internationally important heritage assets. No studies currently exist in the UK incorporating monetary estimates of non-use wetland values. However, some indirect evidence of non-use value is presented in the Broadland wetlands case study below.

## Spatial location and threats

Table 3.2 identifies some of the main UK wetland types, together with the dominant causes of wetland loss, due to either "natural conflicts", market failure or intervention failures.

## "Natural-use" conflicts

The majority of wetland types in the UK (especially estuarine wetlands, salt- and other coastal marshes, and lowland freshwater wetlands) have all come under multiple-use pressure because of their very *spatial location*. Some degree of conflict between wetlands and ongoing economic development processes has, therefore, been inevitable. This conflict can be termed "natural" in that it represents the result of "natural" economic development processes. The history of land reclamation in Belfast Lough illustrates this process. Since 1848, the Lough's wetlands have been destroyed by a combination of shipyard and infrastructure development, together with drainage and landfill disposal activities.

**Table 3.2 Dominant causes of UK wetland losses**

| Selected wetland types and locations | Dominant causes of wetland degradation |
|---|---|
| **Coastal wetlands** | |
| Saltmarshes and estuarine wetlands e.g.Essex Marshes, Morecombe Bay, Mersey Lowlands, The Wash, Tees Bay, Severn Lowlands, Belfast Lough and Foyle, Ribble (Lancs), Orwell (Suffolk). | Agricultural reclamation; industrial/ commercial reclamation (ports, marinas, industrial estates etc.); recreation pressure; pollution waste disposal; potential threat from greenhouse effect and from tidal barrage schemes. |
| Saline marshes; e.g. North Kent Marshes, Dungeness and Romney Marsh, Somerset Levels, Norfolk Broads, Fens. | Agricultural drainage and intensification; pollution on- and off-site; recreation pressure; potential threat from greenhouse effect. |
| **Inland wet meadows and other freshwater wetlands** | |
| e.g. Derwent Ings (Humber Lowlands), Lough Erne Catchment, Suffolk River Valleys, Ouse Washes (Cambridgeshire). | Agricultural drainage and intensification; pollution both on- and off-site; river engineering works. |
| **Inland peatlands** | |
| Upland blanket bog, e.g. Caithness and Sutherland, Cheviots, Scottish Highlands, parts of Northern Ireland, S. Pennines, parts of Wales. | Afforestation; pollution; limited agricultural reclamation; and peat-cutting. |
| Lowland raised bog, e.g. Hatfield Chase, Somerset Levels, parts of Cumbria and Lancashire. | Afforestation; agricultural reclamation and drainage; peat-cutting; waste disposal. |

Note: this is an over-simplified and incomplete classification. Some overlapping of categories exists within the table.

The UK stock of lowland raised bogs and coastal wetlands, especially those near estuarine and port facilities, has been greatly depleted due to a variety of land-use pressures. Estuaries have a number of characteristics that make them attractive for industrial, agricultural and recreational developments. For example, they are flat, they have a freshwater inflow, and they are adjacent to the open sea.

Estuaries on the low coasts of eastern England, from the Humber to North Kent, and in South Wales and north-west England, are all fringed by extensive and fertile saltmarshes. Such areas have been reclaimed for agriculture since Roman times. On the Wash Estuary, for example, some four hundred and seventy square kilometres in total have been enclosed; around 1552 hectares were lost to agriculture between 1960 and 1978.

Much estuarine land has also been claimed for shipping terminals and for the storage and refining of oil, for example Teesmouth (Cleveland), Thames Estuary, Solent (Hampshire), Milford Haven (Wales), and at Nigg Bay on the Cromarty Firth (Scotland). Tidal power barrage schemes have, at one time or another, also been considered for the following estuaries: Severn, Mersey, Humber, Wash, Thames, Dee, Ribble, Morecombe Bay and Solway Firth.

Finally, there are presently proposals for new port developments on the following rivers: Orwell (Suffolk), Stour (Essex), Medway (Kent), Fal (Cornwall), The Dee (Cheshire/Wales), and for Belfast Lough.

## Market failure

*Information failure* has also contributed to the wetland loss process. In the past, there has been a general lack of public appreciation of the full economic value of wetlands kept in a conserved state. The scientific debate over the nature and significance of the conversion processes occurring in UK saltmarshes, for example, has been going on only since the 1960s. Also, the conversion of the Caithness and Sutherland peatlands to afforestation began before any detailed scientific picture of this natural resource had been built up. Incomplete surveys were undertaken by the former UK Nature Conservancy during the 1960s to identify areas meriting protection as National Nature Reserves. But scarce survey resources were then directed at other issues. The launching of more comprehensive vegetational and ornithological surveys of Caithness and Sutherland peatlands during 1979–80 was undertaken only when rapid afforestation was already occurring.

Information failure is also part of the process of destruction afflicting lowland peat wetlands. The last decade or so has seen a large increase in recreational gardening activity, combined with local authority and private sector housing developments. One result has been a massive increase in the sale of peat, through gardening centres, to the general public. In the public- and private-land development sector, there has been an increased emphasis on "green" areas, again requiring significant peat inputs. Large commercial peat-extraction companies have strip-mined lowland peatlands in order to satisfy the market demand. But most of the peat consumers are unaware of this rapid destruction of habitats, or that alternative sources of compost could be developed from wastes such as sewage sludge, domestic household refuse, or tree barks.

Most wetlands in the UK have also suffered, to a greater or lesser extent, from *pollution externality/public good failure*. Lowland and coastal wetlands, in particular, have been degraded because of the impact of *non-point source water pollution*. The run-off of agricultural chemicals, combined with point-source pollution from sewerage waste treatment plants have, for example, inflicted significant damage (eutrophication and loss of species diversity) on the Norfolk and Suffolk Broadlands.

Estuaries have often been used as waste disposal sinks. Wastes discharged there have included fly-ash from coal-fired power stations. This sort of disposal practice has damaged important wader-feeding areas on the Firth of Forth, and others on the Medway (Kent) and Humber estuaries. Mudflat areas in Belfast Lough have also been lost to household waste disposal.

In addition, sewage effluent has affected many estuaries – although it is true that some wildfowl species have actually benefitted from this type of discharge. The Mersey estuary is burdened with some one hundred and thirty-five million gallons of untreated sewage, industrial effluent and surface water run-off every day. Occasional wildlife kills have occurred, for example 2400 birds were killed by alkyl lead discharges from an industrial source into the estuary in 1978–80. However, the bird population does not appear to have been permanently affected, since the estuary is still an internationally important wetland for waterfowl, regularly supporting more than twenty thousand birds.

All upland bogs in the UK are at risk from *acidic air pollution*. A small number, for example those in the southern Pennines hills in England, have suffered severe damage, in terms of altered hydrology, increased soil erosion, and loss of species diversity. This is largely because of their location, downwind of the Manchester–Liverpool conurbation. But other areas may also be at risk as more subtle changes occur, affecting the species composition, and, therefore, the conservation value, of important mire (bog) sites. These peat mires are dominated by bryophytes (sphagnum), which play a major role in determining the physico-chemical structure of the plant community. Unfortunately, these dominant bryophytes are most at risk from atmospheric pollution.

More generally, the overexploitation of the global atmosphere as a waste sink is thought to be responsible for the greenhouse effect, as well as the problem of acid rain. Estimates of possible sea-level rise as a consequence of global warming vary from less than 10 cm to 1.5 m by the year 2050. Scientists working at the University of East Anglia, estimate that, by the year 2050, sea-level will have risen by between 7 and 62 cm above present levels. The best-guess range is 24–38 cm. The rate of rise over the period 1995–2050 is likely to be roughly linear, around 4–6 mm per annum. However, because of a variety of lags, there will be large additional increases in sea-level after 2050, as the systems slowly move toward equilibrium.

The rise in sea-level will produce significant direct impacts, such as changes in coastal erosion and accretion rates; increased frequency of permanent and temporary flooding; and increased saltwater intrusion. All coastal wetlands are potentially at risk, especially those on soft-rock coasts. Mitigation measures, such as raised or new sea walls, barriers and barrages, built primarily to protect industrial/commercial/residential assets, will themselves have consequences for local wetland ecosystems.

As noted above, some wetlands, for example the Broadland and Suffolk River Valleys, yield important *recreational services*. The notion of "carrying capacity" is vital in this context. Recreational benefits are examples of "congestible goods".

There is the danger that recreation-use levels in some wetlands will eventually exceed carrying capacity. This will result in congestion costs and subsequent declines in the quality of both the recreational service and the underlying wetland resource. Restricting the recreational use of wetlands will result in more efficient use only if people who receive the recreation service actually pay for that service. Unfortunately, such economic valuations do not yet exist for UK wetland recreational activities. Furthermore, exclusion is usually not a feasible option. In the Norfolk Broads, for example, water-based recreation pressure is regulated, to some extent, by limits on the number of boat licences issued for commercial hire. There is no similar regulation of private boats. The increased number of boats and the speed at which these boats are driven, both contribute to bank erosion, and to the destruction of bankside vegetation.

The growth of water-based recreation and waterfront housing schemes are also threatening estuarine areas. They have resulted in the loss of wetlands, and in increased disturbances to wildfowl and shorebirds. Most estuaries on the south-east and southern coasts of England have been threatened by marina developments. Langstone Harbour in Hampshire, for example, is under such a threat, but it also supports an average winter maximum of over 7000 Brent geese and 3700 waders – including internationally-important populations of dunlin and black-tailed godwits.

In 1986, a plan was announced for the development of Cardiff docklands, as a work, leisure and housing centre. The plan included a barrage that would enclose the Taff and Ely estuaries, forming a brackish lake about two hundred and sixty hectares in area. This plan would effectively remove the feeding areas for about one per cent of Britain's already-declining overwintering population of redshanks, as well as for a significant proportion of the shelduck, teal and knot which winter on the Severn estuary.

The destruction of some wetlands may also represent permanent removal, that is, *irreversibilities*. This could involve the absolute loss of both existing and future wetland preservation values (preservation value = use value + option value + non-use value). Whether or not the loss of a wetland represents a true irreversibility will depend on the nature and practicability of artificial wetland creation and on restoration possibilities. The artificial creation of a simple wetland, and the partial restoration of a degraded wetland, are quite feasible in many circumstances. For example, man-made sites can compensate for the loss of wetland bird breeding habitat by concentrating breeding waders into relatively small areas such as, for example, Minsmere Reserve in Suffolk, Belfast Harbour Estate, Woodside Road site near Ballymena. Nevertheless, the recreation of complex wetlands, or the full restoration of degraded wetlands may take considerable time, and are both technically difficult and often prohibitively expensive.

## Intervention failure

Due to the absence of an integrated resource management policy, *intersectoral policy inconsistency* has been a feature of UK government interventions in the economic system. The interface between agricultural development policy and wetland conservation is a prime example of this intervention failure. Saline soil marshes and freshwater meadows in the UK are two examples of high-value wetlands which have suffered considerable losses due to conversion to higher intensity agriculture. This conversion process has been artificially stimulated by a wide range of subsidies and price guarantees given to farmers.

For example, until the early 1980s, the UK Ministry of Agriculture, Fisheries and Food (MAFF) operated a system of drainage grants for farmers converting land to higher productivity crops. However, the real driving force behind the historic conversion of UK wetlands has been the high level of intervention prices paid for many crops under the EEC's Common Agricultural Policy (CAP). Within the CAP, cereal intervention prices have at certain times been well above world market prices, for example EEC wheat prices were 40–60 per cent above world market prices over the period 1978–80). The effect of these policies was that the conversion of UK lowland wet grazing meadows into fields of winter wheat became a very profitable financial investment for individual farmers. This financial enticement, combined with public financing of arterial drainage works and government grants for field drainage, have compounded the agricultural overproduction problem, and accelerated the wetland loss rate. The UK MAFF's "departmental view" was that its function was to ensure the *maximum* growth of agricultural output and of agricultural productivity, within the limits of the resources at its disposal. Land drainage and flood protection were seen as strategic instruments for securing those ends, and was therefore subsidized. The MAFF is required to "exercise their functions so as to further conservation", only insofar as this may be consistent with the aims of increased production. Until 1985, UK farmers had also been aided in their land conversions by those agencies who have sponsored flood protection and major arterial drainage schemes, such as Regional Water Authorities and local Internal Drainage Boards. Field drainage schemes which increase farm productivity qualified for a 50 per cent grant from the MAFF. Flood protection and arterial drainage works carried out by Water Authorities and Drainage Boards were also, under certain circumstances, subsidized by MAFF grants.

Another UK public agency, the Nature Conservancy Council (NCC), which does have a nature conservation mandate, *could* be required to compensate farmers who practiced conservation, say, for example, of traditional grazing marshes. Thus, the UK Wildlife and Countryside Acts of 1981 and 1985, helped to protect exceptional conservation assets (SSSI's and nature reserves). However, these laws are still based on *voluntary* codes of conduct, instead of on *statutory* powers and penalties to prevent the destruction of the countryside. The 1981 Act also included provisions for management agreements (between the NCC and landowners) to compensate farmers, when grants for conversion schemes had been refused by the MAFF on conservation grounds. Farmer claims under a management agreement are based on calculations of (financial) profit forgone, due to a continuation of the traditional low-intensity farming practices. Conservation policy, using this particular management approach, is very expensive in financial terms.

A number of analysts have pointed out, however, that the true social costs of conservation are much lower than the financial calculations might indicate (Bowers and Black, 1983; Turner et al., 1983). The legitimate economic costs of conservation are those of forgone agricultural output value, but *minus* the value of agricultural protection in the form of capital grants and price support.

Estimating the precise social value of forgone agricultural output in Europe is complicated by the budgetary flows involved in the CAP system. Restrictions on output affect net budgetary flows, for example between the UK and the EEC, and, hence, the social value of benefit forgone from a UK viewpoint. Two basic methods have been suggested for calculating the social cost of the forgone agricultural output: The Producer Subsidy Equivalents (PSE) method, and the Effective Protection Rate (EPR) method (Willis et al., 1988). The subsidy element varies from year to year and from crop to crop. The PSE method yields higher subsidy estimates than the EPR, but over a period of years, there is no doubt that many intervention crop prices were well above world market prices. At the time of writing (1988–89), the MAFF recommends using a 20 per cent reduction in the value of both beef and cereals outputs, to take account of the implicit subsidy element.

A recent analysis of the net social benefit that might be gained by improving agriculture in three environmentally significant areas (including one wetland site, Derwent Ings) found them to be positive. This means that, for these sites, there is a social cost involved in the conservation option. It is important to remember that, although restrictions on agriculture often do incur *social* costs, this social cost is typically only a fraction of the (apparent) *financial* cost. Thus, without the CAP, the amount of compensation required, assuming free trade in agricultural commodities, to compensate farmers for restrictions on agricultural outputs on significant sites could be considerably less than the present financial guidelines for management agreements outlined by the UK Department of the Environment in 1983 would suggest (Willis and Benson, 1988; Willis et al., 1988).

The coupling of farm income support and production objectives has brought agriculture into conflict with, among others, conservation objectives. The UK compensation system for farmers has resulted in the NCC having to shoulder some of the burden of agricultural support (essentially a MAFF responsibility). The net result is that the financial cost of conservation appears excessive, when it is really agricultural protection which is expensive.

In 1985, the UK government did signal a significant change of policy emphasis, once it recognized that arterial agricultural land drainage schemes provided a low return on investment, coupled with high environmental costs. Consequently, grant-aid has been substantially reduced. Expenditure on land drainage was cut by £12 million to £29.18 million in 1985/86, and further reductions have followed since then. Grant-aid for water authority capital works was reduced from an average of 55 per cent in 1983/84 to 37 per cent in 1985/86; and for internal drainage boards from 50 per cent in 1983/84 to 32 per cent in 1985/86.

Farm capital grant schemes were also modified during the 1980s. Until 1979, field drainage grants under the national Farm Capital Grant Scheme and the EEC-backed Farm and Horticulture Development Scheme, stood at 50 per cent and 60 per cent respectively. These rates were reduced in the early 1980s, and in 1985, national land drainage grants were withdrawn completely. Some farms continued to be eligible for the EEC element of the grant, but only at a reduced rate of 15 per cent.

In Northern Ireland, wetland sites have, over a long period of time, been used as landfill disposal sites. The traditional *waste disposal method* in the UK has been to use landfill sites. Official policy has been underpinned by a "dilute and disperse" philosophy, which has sanctioned the controlled use of so-called "co-disposal" sites. At these locations, certain "special" wastes are landfilled alongside municipal wastes. The majority of landfill sites in England, Wales and Scotland have been located in disused quarries, gravel pits, open-cast mines, and clay pits. In Northern Ireland, however, the District Councils have most often selected wetland sites for the disposal of these wastes (Wells, 1988). Of the 35 disposal sites used by District Councils in 1988, 25 are in wetlands. Of the 50 private waste disposal sites, about 50 per cent are on bog sites.

Although standards of site operation and maintenance vary significantly on mainland Britain, wet sites are generally avoided because of the risk of leachate pollution, and ground- and surface water contamination. The deliberate choice of wetland disposal sites in Northern Ireland is a high risk option with potentially extensive environmental consequences. It is also a direct cause of wetland destruction.

Future waste-management policy in the UK will be orientated more towards a "concentrate and contain" strategy based on "engineered" landfill disposal, at sites selected for their geological and hydrogeological suitability. Such a policy switch is also urgently required in Northern Ireland. Its raised bog wetlands stock has been greatly denuded by a combination of commercial peat extraction, agricultural drainage and waste disposal activities.

*Forestry policy* has been a third major source of intervention failure in the UK. This area of government activity has caused significant destruction of UK blanket bogs. Globally-scarce blanket bog is found extensively in Caithness and Sutherland in Scotland. This area is now under severe threat from coniferous afforestation. The UK Forestry Commission was established in 1919 to rectify Britain's extreme dependency on external timber sources, which far exceeded that of other industrial economies. Since 1950, most of the afforestation programmes have been concentrated in Scotland, in upland Wales, to a more limited extent, and in northern England.

Between 1979 and 1985, private afforestation also expanded rapidly in Scotland. This private expansion was stimulated by both government grants and favourable tax treatment. For example, the development costs of forest plantations can be offset against tax liabilities. This encouraged both higher-income taxpayers and institutions to invest in forestry. (Changes made to the tax regime in 1988, however, reduced the attractiveness of agroforestry as a tax investment.)

## Wetland loss mitigation measures

The UK has deployed a variety of policy instruments over the years in an attempt to conserve its wetland assets. The result is that wetland loss rates were reduced during the 1980s, due to a combination of regulatory, acquisition and management, and incentive policies.

### *Regulation*

Section 28 of the Wildlife and Countryside Acts (1981–5) provides the main protective framework for environmentally valuable habitats. Conservation sites are scheduled and notified as Sites of Special Scientific Interest (SSSI) under the auspices of The Nature Conservancy Council (NCC). This same agency is also charged with the management of National Nature Reserves (NNR). A large number of wetlands or parts of wetlands are protected from development activities because of their SSSI or NNR designation.

The UK is also a signatory to The International Ramsar Convention. Under this convention, several estuarine sites are protected – for example, Bridgewater Bury (Somerset), Lindisfarne (Northumberland), the North Norfolk coast, the Cheshire/Welsh Dee, the River Swale (Kent), the River Alt (Merseyside), and Rockcliffe Marsh (Cumbria). The Alt, Dee, Rockcliffe Marsh and River Ribble (Lancashire) are also designated as Specially Protected Areas under the European Community Directive on the Conservation of Wild Birds (EC 79/409).

General land-use policy in the UK is administered via the Town and Country Planning Acts. However, Private Parliamentary Bills can be used to circumvent this legislation. It was this device which was at the heart of a proposal, in the late 1970s, to construct a tidal barrier at the mouth of the River Yare in Norfolk's Broadland. At the time, the proposal raised a series of objections from environmentalists, and others seeking to conserve the traditional Broads wetlands.

In 1984, a Private Bill was also introduced which sought to expand Felixstowe docks on the River Orwell, Suffolk. The estuary supports an average maximum of 22 000 wintering waders, including internationally important redshanks.

## *Acquisition and management*

Conservation bodies, such as The Royal Society For the Protection of Birds (RSPB), the NCC and the Wildfowl Trust have spent significant amounts of their total budgets on the conservation of wetlands via acquisition. In England and Wales, 7931 ha of wet grassland habitat is under RSPB management; 3025 ha of this was purchased at a total cost of £3.88 million. The RSPB also manages about 13 600 ha of estuarine habitat as reserves. Of this amount, 5180 ha are owned by the Society itself, including large reserves on the Cheshire/Welsh Dee Estuary, Morecombe Bay and the Wash. RSPB records show that it owns a total of 54 wetland reserves.

The NCC manage NNRs on 11 estuaries, including the Wash

and the Ribble. The NCC bought 2200 ha on the Ribble estuary for £1.7 million, before declaring it an NNR. The Wildfowl Trust also has important wildfowl refuges on the Severn and Solway.

It seems reasonable to conclude, however, that land purchase alone will not be sufficient to counter the threat to wetlands from development activities. The resources available to conservation bodies have only been adequate to purchase a small proportion of the land actually under threat of drainage, even if owners were willing to sell (which is not always the case). There are also often technical difficulties. For example, the acquired wetland areas are frequently geographically fragmented, which makes the establishment of viable ecological reserves by purchase or leasing a long-term and difficult process.

## *Incentives*

A policy reorientation which had begun tentatively in 1981, with the passing of the Wildlife and Countryside Act, began to take hold in 1985. In the same year, as noted above, both domestic and EEC capital grants schemes for agricultural "improvement" began to be scaled down. As a consequence, this type of land drainage and wetland conversion was all but halted.

Also in 1985, a scheme known as the Broads Grazing Marshes Conservation Scheme (BGMCS) was introduced, on a pilot basis until 1988, in the Norfolk Broads. The BGMCS was a response to an ongoing "conservation-versus-development" conflict centred on the Halvergate marshes. These marshes represent a strategic part of the last remaining extensive stretch of open-grazing marsh in eastern England. This case is also interesting, because, for nine months of the year, the Halvergate marshes are practically inaccessible, and, even in summer, visitation rates are insignificant. Non-use values (existence and bequest) are therefore presumably very important. It is also likely that conservationists saw this dispute as a political "test case".

In 1986, Broadland and five other areas were designated as Environmentally Sensitive Areas (ESAs). As of 1989, there were some 13 ESAs in the UK, several of which (for example the Broads, the Somerset Levels, Suffolk River Valleys) are important wetlands. Both the ESA and BGMC schemes offered financial incentives to farmers who chose to follow a set of management guidelines designed to promote traditional land uses. Thus, conversion of land to arable regimes – which requires deep drainage – was discouraged in favour of low-intensity summer grazing regimes (high water table). In this way, both the landscape and the ecological aspects of wetlands can be conserved on a sustainable-use basis.

Almost all UK grazing marshes (freshwater and saline) have suffered significant losses due to intensive conversion of agricultural land. In their semi-natural state, these wetlands support floristically-rich and diverse natural grasslands. The freshwater dyke systems form a valuable habitat for aquatic plants, insects and amphibians, some of which are of national or international importance. The marshes are also important breeding grounds for wading birds. Traditional practices such as low-intensity grazing, reed cultivation, and controlled waterfowl hunting, are largely compatible with the maintenance of the semi-natural wetland ecosystem structure.

The conversion of these marshes to intensive livestock or arable cropping, which typically requires drainage and a significant lowering of the water table, effectively destroys the marsh habitat. Both the dyke systems and their flora and fauna, as well as the overall landscape amenity, become degraded. Over a period of time, even the surviving areas of original marshland become adversely affected by nutrient enrichment, due to run-off pollution from the converted areas. Within some of the converted marshes, particularly in Kent, soil productivity and structural loss problems have recently come to light. These latter problems, together with the pollution run-off damage, cast doubts on the long-term sustainability of the intensive agricultural land-use option for these wetlands.

The ESA concept has its origin in EEC Regulation No. 797/85, introduced in March 1985 as part of a package of measures designed to mitigate the twin problems of farm income maintenance and surplus production. Article 19 of the Regulation enables member states to designate ESAs. For the purpose of this Regulation, there are "areas of recognised importance from ecological and landscape point of view". Member state governments may make available grant-aid to farmers who undertake to farm environmentally important areas so as to preserve or improve the environment. Regulation 797/85 is, nevertheless, primarily a means of persuading farmers to reduce agricultural production, rather than a conservation measure *per se*.

## The Norfolk and Suffolk Broadland case

Broadland represents a "class one" complex wetland because it is recognized as providing a wide range of functional and structural values. Broadland is, therefore, of considerable significance for wetland conservation. There are three National Nature Reserves within it – Bure Marshes, Hickling Broad, and Ludham Marshes, the first two of which appear on the list of wetlands recognized by the British government (under the Ramsar Convention), as being of international importance. In addition, there are 24 SSSIs, with more due to be so designated in the near future. The Broadland fens support reed- and sedge-beds and companion fauna. The grazing marshes support important wildfowl populations, and their drainage dykes contain over a hundred different species of freshwater plants. Broadland was specifically designated an "Environmentally Sensitive Area" under the Agriculture Act of 1986.

### *Ecosystem change and management in Broadland*

The Broadland wetlands also provide for multiple-resource use and encompass multiple land-use systems. The area is a national centre for recreation. It supports a regionally important agriculture industry; a substantial permanent population; as well as a large seasonal tourist population. The origins of the Broads lie in the flooding of medieval peat-diggings; in the connection of these shallow lakes to the main watercourses; and in the creation of a marsh-based economy. Today, this semi-natural area supports a variety of intensive and extensive agricultural land uses on the pump-drained marshland. The combination of chalky soils and agricultural activities yields a significant impact on the chemical composition of the water draining into the waterways. The result is that the lower reaches of the river and some downstream Broads are both affected by saline intrusions. Relatively small changes in rates of sewage effluent discharge, or in extractions (for example, for spray irrigation and residential consumption purposes) can quickly alter water quality levels. Undrained wetlands are located on peat soils in the upper parts of the valley, while the drained marshes and arable lands lie below the level of the waterway, usually behind clay-peat embankments.

The management of Broadlands has proven to be a complex task, and several factors have helped to intensify land-use conflicts over recent years. Figure 3.1 summarizes the main factors leading to ecosystem change in the area, as well as the resulting socio-economic implications, and inherent conflicts resulting from these changes.

Increasing demands on the productive use of wetland resources – such as for increased agricultural output; for more recreation; and for more water for consumption and/or effluent assimilation – have created undesirable side-effects. There has been an accelerated enrichment of the watercourses by nutrients (eutrophication), which has, in turn, led to algal growth and decay, and to the associated loss of vegetation, and to organic decay. Changes in the characteristic landscape of the area have also been stimulated; loss of reed-banks; channelization and quay-heading of river banks; loss of grazing marsh and of related dyke habitats; and loss of natural ornithological and invertebrate attributes.

## *Water quality and bank erosion*

Under natural conditions, reed-beds (the rand) and other aquatic vegetation act as a buffer to protect the river banks from erosion (caused by boat wash and wind-driven waves). The flood defences in the region consist primarily (but not exclusively) of clay banks, which are "soft defences", often on unstable foundations. Where the natural reed-beds have deteriorated, or been destroyed, the river banks have frequently been piled with timber or sheet steel. The cost of river-wall maintenance has become increasingly burdensome, and it is now averaging around £250 per metre of bank. There has been a gradual loss of the protective reed rand in recent times, due to both water quality deterioration (eutrophication), and to physical damage.

While nitrate concentrations in the Broadland river systems have increased significantly in the last 40 years, loadings of

**Figure 3.1 Ecosystem change and environmental management in Broadland**

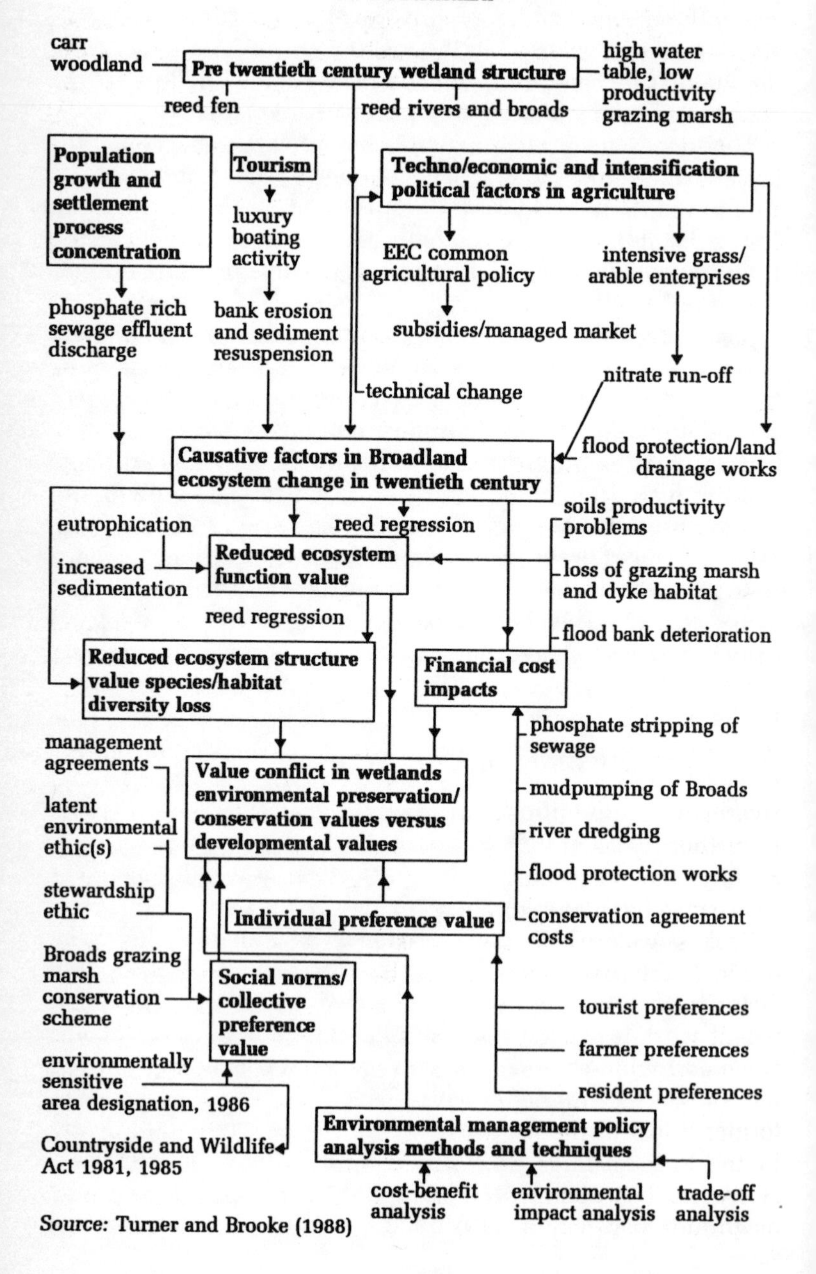


*Source:* Turner and Brooke (1988)

potassium have not changed very much. It is thought that this high nitrogen to potassium ratio in the Broads' waterways detrimentally affects floating reedswamp, and may similarly affect reed rooted in sediment. Research into reed regression has shown that such conditions lead to a weakening of the root and rhizome biomass, critical to the stability of the reed-bed. High nitrate loadings also promote short growth rather than the growth of rhizomes and roots, thereby contributing to a reduction of the tissues which strengthen both reed and rhizome. A less substantial root must, therefore, support the structural integrity of the reed-bed, and the reed itself is less able to withstand physical damage.

Thus, the stability and the effectiveness of the Broads' river banks is now extensively threatened. The initial response to the nutrient-enrichment process was a lush growth of river plants. By the mid 1960s, however, high nutrient loadings had led to further changes. Algae thrived, turning the water cloudy, and preventing sunlight from reaching the bottom of the river. Partly as the result of this process, the submerged plants, which also help to buffer the flood bank against erosion, have also been lost from most of the Broads' waterways.

Physical damage to riverside vegetation, and to the flood embankments themselves, pose another problem. The careless trampling of this vegetation by recreationists may contribute to the exposure of the riverbank, making it more susceptible to erosion. Another likely problem is the deliberate cutting of vegetation by a small number of anglers. The grazing of riverbanks by wildfowl, and until recently by coypu, leads to further losses of the vegetation protecting the embankment. Finally, the persistent mooring of boats against unprotected riverbanks has also taken its toll.

Broads waterways are extensively used by holiday boat traffic. In the past, boat traffic has been cited as a probable major factor in the growing problem of riverbank erosion. However, recent work investigating the likely significance of both boat-wave and wind-generated wave energy in the erosion process has shown that the latter is more significant overall than the former. Most of the boat-wave contribution to the problem is in the form of large numbers of waves of small amplitude. However, boatwash wave energy increases by an order of magnitude between speeds of 5 and 7 mph, and variations in traffic density have also been found to have a significant effect on the amount of boat-wave energy in some reaches.

Therefore, opportunities to redesign hull configurations are now being investigated, with a long-term objective of reducing boat-wash and bank erosion. As an interim measure, it would seem sensible to reduce the speed limits for boats (currently set at 7 mph), particularly if it is confirmed that the larger waves (above 75 mm) associated with boatwash *do* contribute significantly to bank erosion.

## *Yare barrier controversy*

In the past, financial pressures persuaded some farmers to drain some of the pumped marshlands, and convert them from low intensity grazing regimes into intensive arable production. As a result, much characteristic grazing marsh landscape is being lost. Associated with this trend is a loss in the ecological importance of the (previously high water level) drainage dykes and ditches. A simultaneous loss of ornithological and invertebrate value has also occurred.

The Broadland system is subject to periodic saltwater flooding, especially when surge conditions in the North Sea coincide with high tides. Such a combination of surge tide and storm conditions caused a major flooding event in the North Sea Basin in 1953. During the 1970s, the regional water authority proposed to construct a flood barrier across the River Yare specifically to deal with such storm/surge flood events, which at the time were estimated to have a return period of between one in 100 and one in 175 years.

A number of official cost-benefit studies of the barrier project were undertaken on behalf of the water authority. The results of these official studies caused a storm of controversy, and were challenged by a variety of interest groups. The scheme opponents were able to demonstrate that even on narrow economic-efficiency grounds, the net present value of the barrier project was negative. They also showed that, when wider environmental criteria were added, significant environmental damage would result from the project.

More specifically, opponents demonstrated that a significant percentage of the scheme's benefits – increased levels of arable crop output, and improved grazing regime values because of new drainage and land conversion activities, supplemented by added "insurance" against flood risk – yielded negative economic returns.

Environmental assessments then demonstrated the extent of the ecological, especially drainage-dyke flora and fauna, and landscape asset losses that the barrier would have caused. They also highlighted the extent of an acid-sulphate soils problem in several areas which would mitigate against arable cultivation. They pointed out that the presence of an acid layer in the soil would reduce crop yields, and would necessitate remedial soil treatments. The overall result would be an increase in variable costs, and reduced gross margins.

More recently, another soil quality problem has been identified in the region. A few areas of marsh are suffering from saline deflocculation, first identified in Britain on the North Kent marshes. Available treatments, such as the application of large amounts of ground gypsum, and the jetting of the underdrainage network, are very expensive. Additional costs of between £10 per ha, where the soils are carefully managed, and preventative measures are taken, and £150 per ha, where the problem is severe and well-established, would significantly reduce the potential net returns from arable crops on these soils.

Because of the uncertainties involved, estimating the monetary value of wetland functions and services has proved to be a formidable task. However, the Broadlands case suggests that there is still an important and constructive role for an incomplete (economic-efficiency) analysis in the wetlands exploitation context (Turner and Brooke, 1988; Pearce and Turner, 1989). An important element of such an analysis, given that an estimate of the direct total economic value of a wetland will usually not be available, would be an estimate of the likely *economic opportunity costs of wetland conservation*. In effect, the opportunity cost of (unpriced) wetland services can be estimated from the forgone income of potential development uses.

In the case of Broadland Marshes in Norfolk, more intensive agricultural use is the only feasible development option. Studies undertaken in the UK (Bowers, 1983; Turner et al., 1983) suggest that such schemes have often produced negative net benefits. Therefore, the social opportunity cost of conservation, that is, the cost of retaining the area as wetland, is unlikely to be very high, and may even be zero. Critics of the UK land drainage investment programme have argued that such conversion of wetlands would have occurred even without many of the subsidized capital works, because of the extra financial returns available to arable farmers under the EEC Common Agricultural Policy. The correct benefits in such cases should, therefore, be limited to those benefits which would be derived from an *accelerated* take-up by farmers, as well as to consequent improvements in crop yields. It is likely that these benefits would be relatively small, and that negative economic returns would often be generated by such schemes.

This negative conclusion would be further reinforced if the analysis also took account of the loss of environmental assets inherent in the conversion process, and of the fact that a residual flooding risk is still present in the area. On the other hand, a more recent study by Willis et al. (1988) has shown that, in some cases (for example Derwent Ings), there are positive social costs associated with wetland conservation.

The barrier scheme, and its concept of uniform area-wide flood protection, was finally shelved by the Water Authority in the early 1980s. Nevertheless, large tracts of marshes had by then been drained and converted. On a more positive note, the use of CBA by both sides in the conflict did lead to a clarification of many of the issues involved, and also (over time) reduced factual misunderstandings.

## *Management agreements in Broadland*

Both the BGMCS and the ESA scheme in Broadland were compromise arrangements that have subsequently proven to be of benefit to both farmers and conservationists. The ESA scheme has been popular with farmers. The scheme offers payments of between £125 and £200 per ha, depending on the severity of the restrictions imposed upon agricultural management practices. By 1988, the BGMCS had been cancelled, and the associated marshes became eligible for entry into the ESA. About six hundred farmers had chosen to sign voluntary five-year management agreements with the MAFF.

Approximately eleven thousand nine hundred hectares are now being farmed, using specified extensive, low-input livestock systems (57 per cent of the total agricultural average, or 85 per cent of the existing grassland average within the scheme boundaries). By 1988, some three thousand hectares in the scheme had been entered in "Tier II", the most restrictive category in terms of management rules, and hence the most beneficial for ecological and landscape amenity conservation (table 3.3). Farmers entering the scheme must agree to maintain a permanent grassland, initially for five years, and to abide by regulations governing the number and types of stock kept, the number of cuts of hay or silage taken, the amount of nitrogen applied, and the water levels maintained in the drainage area.

**Table 3.3: Selected statistics for the Broads ESA area**

| Land use in ESA area (ha.) | | Scheme take-up (Oct 1988) | |
|---|---|---|---|
| Total scheme average | 29 870 | Number of agreements | 599 |
| Existing grassland | 13 961 | Average in Tier I | 8932 |
| Existing arable | 6617 | Average in Tier II | 2955 |
| Wet fen | 2497 | Total in scheme | 11 887 |
| Woodland | 3313 | % take up in Tier I | 75 |
| Open water | 885 | % take up in Tier II | 25 |
| Other (urban, roads, etc.) | 2597 | Average size of agreement area (ha) | 22.9 |

*Source*: Brooke and Turner (1989)

The ESA scheme has also allowed an indirect valuation of the wetland's landscape and wildlife aspects to be undertaken. The method used is based on an extended interpretation of neo-classical economics assumptions about "rational economic man". Specifically, it is based on the argument that individuals can express *public-preference values*, as well as the more conventional *private-preference* (willingness-to-pay) *values*. Such collective or "community regarding" values are linked to social norms and operationalized via legislation and rules. These values are not static, and they evolve over time.

In this context, payments to farmers under the ESA schemes are, in a certain sense, an approximation of per hectare social value, pragmatically expressed through the workings of the political system. They are payments representing an approximate minimum value to society of the landscape and wildlife asset (of £125 to £200 per ha).

## Flood alleviation policy

Broadland remains under continued threat from flooding, some twenty thousand hectares lying below the surge tide level. This area is protected by over two hundred kilometres of tidal embankments in a deteriorating condition. By the mid-1980s, various pieces of scientific evidence had become available, all of which indicated that the risk of flooding in the Broadland area was probably increasing over time. In the aftermath of major flood damage in 1953, a substantial investment was made in flood protection works for the entire east coast of England. Most of these works have a maximum design life of 30–50 years, and many existing defences are now reaching the end of their useful life. The current standard of flood protection provided by the river walls in Broadland is frequently below a one in ten- (or even a one in five-) year return period level on the river.

On the assumption that some overall level of flood protection (from saline inundation) for Broadland is essential, cost-effectiveness analysis, rather than cost-benefit analysis, is now being used to plan a *selective flood protection strategy*. The strategy has multiple goals, and encompasses an economic analysis which is being run in parallel with environmental impact investigations, in order to determine priority areas for protection. Selectivity is therefore interpreted in a number of dimensions – economic, environmental and aesthetic/ethical. Within the overall strategy, the costs of alternative means of achieving given levels of flood protection are being compared with damage-cost-avoided measures of benefits for agricultural, residential/industrial and environmental assets (Turner and Brooke, 1988; Brooke and Turner, 1989).

## Conclusions on Broadlands

The increased government intervention encapsulated in schemes such as the BGMCS and ESA will reduce the impact of recent changes of the agriculture grant-aid system. ESA designation for the Broads, with its potential to manage the area for dual objectives, should also help to stimulate the formulation of sustainable wetland management guidelines. A combination of subtle pressures for change and some measure of economic incentives can be seen to be operative within the ESA policy.

The proposed selective flood-protection strategy for Broadland also indicates that conservation interests can be accommodated within public agency policy, despite overall public expenditure constraints. Neither outright public purchases, nor voluntary management agreements are likely to provide sufficiently extensive protection. In any case, these policies would be prohibitively expensive. Government intervention via a package of conservation incentive instruments centred around a core of regulatory change is likely to be the most cost-effective strategy. Most recently (1989), the Broads have been given virtual national park status, and the powers of the management agency have been strengthened and extended. Clearly, these are steps in the right direction.

## The case of Caithness and Sutherland peatlands

These wetlands represent the largest area of actively-growing acid bog (an internationally-rare habitat) in Britain. Their vegetation is composed of plant communities which have counterparts only in Ireland, where significant losses have already occurred. The high degree of surface "patterning", or pool formation, on the flatter areas of peatland ("flows") is of particular conservation significance (NCC, 1987). The pools support a specialized range of mosses and vascular plants and they provide essential feeding habitats for wetland birds.

These blanket bogs support a particularly varied northern type of bird fauna not found in identical composition elsewhere in the world (table 3.4). Many of the breeding bird species on these peatlands are listed in Annex 1 of the EEC's Directive on the Conservation of Wild Birds. The peatlands also meet the agreed criteria of internationally important wetlands under the Ramsar Convention.

Of all terrestrial habitats in Britain, these blanket bogs are the largest example of a primaeval ecosystem. They are of global significance, with both structural and biological features peculiar to Britain. The peatlands' significance lies in their total extent; in their continuity; in their diversity (as mire forms and vegetation complexes); and in the total size and species

**Table 3.4: Estimated proportions of national and EEC populations of selected bird species breeding in the Caithness and Sutherland (C&S) peatlands**

| | Estimated C&S breeding population (pairs) | Estimated British breeding population (pairs) | Proportion of British population on C&S peatlands (%) | Proportion of European Communities' population on C&S peatlands (%) |
|---|---|---|---|---|
| Red-throated diver | 150 | 1000–1200 | 14 | 14 |
| Black-throated diver | 30 | 50 | 20 | 20 |
| Greylag goose | c.300 | 600–800 | 43 | |
| Widgeon | 80 | 300–500 | 20 | 20 |
| Common scoter | 30+ | 75–80 | 39 | 16 |
| Hen harrier | 30 | 600 | 5 | 1 |
| Golden eagle | 30 | 510 | 6 | <1 |
| Merlin | 30 | 600 | 5 | 4 |
| Peregrine | 35 | 730 | 5 | <1 |
| Golden plover | 3980 | 22 600 | 18 | 17 |
| Temminck's stint | <10 | <10 | | |
| Dunlin | 3830 | 9900 | 39 | 35 |
| Ruff | <10 | 10–12 | | |
| Greenshank | 630 | 960 | 66 | 66 |
| Wood sandpiper | <10 | 1–12 | | |
| Red-necked phalarop | <10 | 19–24 | | |
| Arctic skua | 60+ | 2800 + | 2 | 2 |
| Short-eared owl | 50 | 1000 + | 5 | 4 |

Source: NCC (1987)

composition of their bird populations.

Until the 1970s, the region had largely escaped the more intensive kinds of land use, because of its remote location. Its nature conservation assets had been retained under a combination of traditional management for low-intensity sheep farming, some sporting activities (shooting and fishing), and local small-scale peat extraction. In recent years, however, coniferous afforestation, run by state and private enterprise, has been destroying these peatlands. Until the 1970s, blanket bogs covered some four hundred thousand hectares of Caithness and Sutherland. By the mid-1980s, 80 000 ha had been lost to forestry, which requires deep ploughing and drainage. These requirements adversely affect water tables and surface flow patterns, and, over the long run, can result in erosion, shrinkage, deep cracking and oxidation of peat. After 10–15 years, the forest becomes so dense that ground vegetation is eliminated. The peatland loss is virtually an irreversible process.

Afforestation produces both localized and more widespread environmental impacts. The original peatland bird assemblage is replaced by a woodland mix, which is considered to be of lower conservation assemblage value. Neither the ground vegetation nor the bird assemblage show more than insignificant recovery to original states during subsequent clearance phases in the forest rotation process. In the early stages of plantation development, the impacts of afforestation include increased sediment loads in watercourses; faster rates of water run-off; and other hydrological changes. Some eutrophication is also possible. Both the quality of the breeding habitat for water birds and freshwater fisheries can be adversely affected.

The Caithness and Sutherland peatlands meet all eight of the Ramsar Convention criteria for wetlands of international importance, and should be viewed as an integrated ecosystem. It is possible to undertake a limited number of activities in this ecosystem on a sustainable basis, but forestry is not one of them. The irreversible loss of the peatland and its replacement with a much lower rank – in nature conservation terms – woodland ecosystem, represents a net loss of social value. The forestry activity is as much a response to fiscal opportunities as it is to the economic/strategic needs of the economy. To emphasize this point, one need only realize that the budgetary changes of 1988 greatly reduced the attractiveness of forestry developments in the area from the private investor's viewpoint. The essential point is that the "flow" peatlands represent rare habitat, both nationally and globally. Forestry, even if judged to be socially desirable, could be undertaken in a wide range of other geographic zones. It need not impinge on rare peatland habitats.

## The case of Northern Ireland

Northern Ireland receives a large amount of rainfall, and has soils of low permeability, derived predominantly from boulder clays and peats, which are often waterlogged in their natural state. Given these conditions, wetlands are a predominant feature of the Province's landscape. The wetlands range from numerous small interdrumlin fens and raised bogs, to open water sites and rivers with wet grasslands in the floodplain. These wetlands support wintering wildfowl populations of international significance. Northern Ireland's wetlands have been disappearing at a rapid rate during the twentieth century, especially since the 1930s. The main causes of wetland loss and degradation have been:

- agricultural land drainage and conversion schemes;
- waste disposal practices;
- commercial peat extraction; and
- industrial land reclamation.

The Lower Bann Drainage Scheme, for example, eliminated some fifty-seven thousand hectares of wetland around Lough Neagh between 1930 and 1940. After 1945, arterial and field drainage schemes continued to expand. Since 1947, well over half of the total agricultural land of Northern Ireland has come under some kind of field drainage. In the process, about eighty-nine per cent of lowland peat (raised bogs), and twenty-three per cent of upland blanket peat in Northern Ireland has been destroyed, or greatly modified. This generally represents a major loss of conservation value, although the habitat for some bird species, for example waders, has occasionally been improved.

## *Agricultural land drainage*

Agriculture is of proportionately greater significance to the Northern Ireland economy than it is in the rest of the UK. Approximately five per cent of Northern Ireland's gross domestic product is derived from that sector. About ten per cent of the Northern Ireland workforce is engaged on farms and a further three per cent work in ancillary industries directly dependent on agriculture. Political support for drainage and agricultural improvement schemes has, therefore, been very strong. Since 1947, about £200 million has been spent on all types of drainage. Arterial drainage works are organized under the Drainage (NI) Order of 1973. In contrast with the situation in England and Wales, these activities are the direct responsibility of a single government department – the Drainage Division of the Department of Agriculture for Northern Ireland (DANI).

The rate of field drainage increased markedly during the late 1970s, and increased even more sharply with the introduction of the special Agriculture Development Programme (ADP) established under EEC Regulation 1942/81. This provided higher grants for capital works – such as farm drainage – within the less favoured areas of Northern Ireland.

Drainage operations result in the loss of wetland habitat and detrimental effects on wetland fauna. These impacts are compounded by the agricultural intensification which occurs after drainage. Intensification has led to pollution of watercourses by slurry and silage effluents, damaging invertebrates, fisheries and birdlife. Drainage improvements have also facilitated the early cutting of grass for silage. This practice has been identified as a contributory factor in the decline of the corncrake.

Land drainage has posed a major threat to the wetlands of Fermanagh and the Erne Catchment. The Lough Erne catchment has long been recognized by conservation agencies as an internationally important area for birds. The conservation values of the upper Lough Erne combine with extensive lowland pastoral agriculture to produce an impressive range of habitats for wetland birds. The corncrake is the first priority for wildbird conservation in the Erne Catchment. But the basin also compares favourably with major wetland sites in Great Britain for breeding waders and wintering wildfowl. It ranks third in overall importance in the UK, after the Somerset Levels and the North Kent marshes.

The farms of the area are mainly small, and are dominated by beef and dairy enterprises. Many farmers have intensified their land management in recent years with hedge removal, substitution of silage for hay, and the building of housed units to facilitate intensive production. Traditional late-season cutting of hay, which has declined, at one time helped to maintain the type of fields favoured by breeding corncrakes.

In addition, cross-border arterial drainage schemes have been promoted by the EEC. Under EEC Directive 79/197, the governments of the UK and Eire were permitted to spend £15 million EC units of account (£11 million) on an approved programme of cross-border drainage schemes. Some 50 per cent of this expenditure would be refunded from the European Agricultural Guidance and Guarantee Fund. Two schemes were submitted to the Commission for approval: the Blackwater and the Finn-Lackey, to improve the drainage of 3200 ha and 1400 ha of agricultural land in Northern Ireland respectively.

The Blackwater Improvement Scheme is a major drainage undertaking, to be phased in over several years. The Blackwater was once an attractive river, gravel-bedded, sinuous and lined with earth cliffs, alder, oak and ash woodland. It was also an important game-fishing river and a range of bird species and otters were often seen along its length. The floodplain was dotted by small wetlands important for breeding waders, especially snipe and lapwings. In winter, flood waters attracted whooper swans and Greenland white-fronted geese.

As a result of the channel-deepening works, most river channel habitats have been now been lost. In the floodplain, watercourses have been deepened to provide farmers with adequate outfalls for field drainage. By early 1985, it was apparent that the project's design had paid insufficient attention to the soils of the catchment and, as a result, the newly constructed channel was very unstable. As the river adjusted to its new regime, there was considerable bank erosion, causing the further loss of trees. In an attempt to stabilize the river, further ecological damage was caused, and this cancelled out the beneficial effect of some of the previous conservation measures. There has been a substantial reduction in breeding populations of river birds since 1984, the impact of the scheme being particularly severe on those species requiring aquatic vegetation.

The Finn-Lacky Scheme, as proposed, is intended to improve the drainage of 1400 ha of agricultural land in Northern Ireland. The total cost of the scheme would be £5.5 million (1987 prices). Approximately one hundred and thirty-five kilometres of watercourses would be widened and deepened, to increase channel capacity, to reduce flooding, and to give a freeboard sufficient to permit the installation of fold drainage.

The Finn-Lacky catchment has significant conservation value. It is an example of a now rare, pristine lowland river, meandering across a floodplain, and locked between drumlins. The catchment is also of considerable ornithological interest, supporting breeding waders and a rich riparian bird community. In winter, the Finn Floods have had over one thousand wildfowl. As proposed, the scheme works threaten both the river's exceptional physiographical features, and its conservation importance as a wetland.

## *Waste disposal*

Wetland sites have frequently been used as landfill sites in Northern Ireland. The loss of wetland habitat is compounded by potential water pollution impacts beyond the site, affecting both surface and groundwater supplies. Waste disposal activities also attract large gull populations. These birds can have negative impacts on areas up to 20 miles from the landfill. Rare tern colonies, for example, are reported to have been damaged by gulls. Currently, about 166 ha of mudflat, 102 ha of cut-over raised bog, and 32 ha of swamp/mixed fen are being used by District Councils for the disposal of waste in Northern Ireland (Wells, 1988).

The tipping of municipal solid waste on to, for example, a raised bog, completely destroys the habitat. Adjacent areas of peatland are also affected, as nitrogen levels are increased by leaching. This leads to the eutrophication of neighbouring sections of the bog, and an eventual decline in species diversity. Examples of particularly important wetlands degraded by landfill operations include the mudflats in Belfast Lough, Lough Foyle wetland and an interdrumlin bog area around Eskragh Lough near Dungannon.

## *Future prospects*

Nature conservation in Northern Ireland is the responsibility of the Countryside and Wildlife Branch of the Department of the Environment (NI). This Branch carries out the work that in Britain is done by the NCC and the Countryside Commission. Conservation has traditionally had a low profile in Northern Ireland. This had led to information failure in that there is a serious lack of basic wildlife survey information. Because of this data deficiency a number of important sites (many of them wetlands) have undoubtedly been unknowingly damaged by reclamation and waste disposal activities.

Intersectoral policy inconsistency is very evident in Northern Ireland, with intervention failures being especially damaging to wetlands in the context of waste disposal and agricultural improvement policies.

Agricultural drainage operations, both within Northern Ireland and across the border with Eire, have been substantial, and the environmental cost has been high. In part, this has been due to pressure from the farming community for drainage schemes, as a means of increasing the agricultural productivity of their land. However, until 1986, the full social economic value of these schemes had not been quantified (another form of information failure). Scheme appraisals were limited to "in-house" DANI analysis, based largely on engineering and some financial (private cost) criteria. Appraisal data was not routinely released, and no independent verification of the cost-benefit analysis was possible.

The statutory notification of Wetland sites as Areas of Special Scientific Interest (ASSI) under the Amenity Lands (NI) Act of 1965, has done little to limit the loss of wetlands due to drainage activities. This is so, both because the designation process offers little actual protection for wetlands, and because few sites were notified (51 during the life of the Act, of which only nine were inland wetlands). Many important wetlands have no statutory designation protection, for example the Blackwater Catchment; Finn-Lacky floodplain; Lough Neagh; and Lough Erne Catchment.

The passing of the Nature Conservation and Amenity Lands (NI) Order 1985 (the equivalent of Britain's 1981 Wildlife and Countryside Act), significantly increased the protection afforded to sites, once they have been designated as ASSIs. Few sites, however, had been notified by 1988, only one of which was a wetland (Lough Beg).

Under the 1985 Order, DANI is required to "have regard" for countryside conservation and "to protect (so far as reasonably practicable) flora, fauna, geological and physiographical features from any harmful effects which may result from the exercise of [its] functions". Moreover, the Drainage (NI) Order 1973 requires DANI to provide "protection" for any fishery that may be affected by its works. DANI's Drainage Division is, however, not bound, as English and Welsh drainage authorities are, by a positive duty "to further" the conservation of flora and fauna, consistent with the overall objectives of a scheme.

In the long term, successful wetland conservation in Northern

Ireland will require more than the reform of land drainage financial and administrative practices. Promising signs of this trend have, however, been evident since 1986. It will also require the establishment of farming regimes which integrate nature conservation with agricultural objectives. The designation of Environmentally Sensitive Areas could provide a useful step in this direction. Funding is now available for ESAs from the European Commission – to cover 25 per cent of costs.

The merits of designating the Erne Catchment as an ESA have recently been reviewed (Corkindale, 1988). It has been suggested that, rather than paying farmers to adopt conservation practices via financial compensation for lost agricultural output, it may be more appropriate to pay a fixed sum on the basis of monitored conservation results. Thus, in the Erne Catchment, there are many important breeding sites for birds. For example, farmers could be paid a fixed sum for each pair of breeding birds nesting on their land.

Corkindale has noted that DANI proposes to make £300 000 per annum available for the Mournes Mountains ESA, at a rate of £30 per hectare. If a similar total sum (£300 000 per annum) were available for conserving the 1524 pairs of breeding waders in the Lough Erne Catchment, this would imply a payment of just under £197 per pair. Such a payment (proxy social-preference value) would be a far more powerful incentive to the farmer to conserve breeding waders than a payment of £30 per hectare of land farmed under ESA management guidelines.

## References

Armentano, T. V. and E. S. Menges, "Patterns of Change in the Carbon Balance of Organic Soil Wetlands of the Temperate Zone", *Journal of Ecology*, vol. 74, pp.755–74 (1986).

Bowers, J. K., "Cost-benefit analysis of wetland drainage", *Environment and Planning*, vol. 15, pp.227–35 (1983).

Brooke, J. and R. K. Turner, *A Selective Flood Alleviation Strategy for Broadland: Draft Final Report to Anglian Water Environmental Appraisal Group* (Norwich: University of East Anglia, 1989).

Corkindale, J., *A Conservation Strategy for the Erne Catchment* (Sandy (Beds): Royal Society for the Protection of Birds, 1988).

Institute of Terrestrial Ecology (ITE), *Climate Change, Rising Sea Level and the British Coast* (London: HMSO, 1989).

Moss, B., "The Broads", *Biologist*, vol. 34, pp.7–13 (1987).

Nature Conservancy Council, *Birds, Bogs and Forestry: the Peatlands of Caithness and Sutherland* (Peterborough, 1987).

Pearce, D. W. and R. K. Turner, *Economics of Natural Resources and the Environment* (Hemel Hempsted: Harvester Wheatsheaf, 1989).

Royal Society for the Protection of Birds, *Conservation Review* (Sandy (Beds): 1987).

Turner, R. K. and J. Brooke, "Management and Valuation of an Environmentally Sensitive Area: Norfolk Broadland, England, Case Study", *Environmental Management*, vol. 12, pp.19–20 (1988).

Turner, R. K., D. Dent and R. D. Hey, "Valuation of the Environmental Impact of Wetland Flood Protection and Drainage Schemes", *Environment and Planning A*, vol. 15, pp.871–88 (1983).

Wells, J., *Waste Disposal and Conservation in Northern Ireland* (Sandy (Beds): Royal Society for the Protection of Birds, 1988).

Willis, K., J. Benson and C. Saunders, "The Impact of Agricultural Policy on the Costs of Nature Conservation", *Land Economics*, vol. 64, pp.147–57 (1988).

Willis, K. and J. Benson, "Valuation of Wildlife. A Case Study on the Upper Teesdale Site of Special Scientific Interest and Comparison of Methods in Environmental Economics" in: Turner, R. K. (ed.), *Sustainable Environmental Management: Principles and Practice* (London: Belhaven Press, 1988).

# 4

# FRANCE

Laurent Mermet

## French wetlands: an overview

When reviewing French wetland policy, it is important to keep two important characteristics of the French environment in mind. The first of these relates to the *broad geographic diversity* of France – a diversity which is large by European standards, in terms of both its natural conditions and its development history. This diversity is also reflected in France's wetland environments. The northwestern part of the country contains wetlands reminiscent of those in England, Belgium, and Holland. Northeastern wetlands resemble more those of Central Europe – in particular, Germany, and Austria. In the South, the ecological conditions are closer to those of Spain or Greece. Finally, the numerous mountain regions possess their own wetland types and specific environmental problems. Understanding this diversity is fundamental to understanding French wetlands.

The second important characteristic concerns is the *high level of transformation by human activity* that most French wetlands have undergone in the past millennium. There is virtually no wetland in France which is not already a significant part of the rural economic fabric. As a result, people have used, managed, or transformed almost the entire wetland environment over time. This situation is very different from that in less densely populated countries, such as those of Scandinavia or North America. This high degree of human intervention has also left a significant mark on the country's political response to wetlands management problems.

There is no specific wetland policy in France. Wetlands are only taken into account within the framework of more general environmental management policies. As a result, only wetlands of particular environmental interest are listed in a computerized national inventory of areas with special flora or fauna characteristics. These are called "Zones Naturelles d'Intérêt Ecologique, Faunistique et Floristique".

There is no general inventory of French wetlands as such, but there are several more specialized inventories, each serving a more specific purpose. For example, Leduc (unpublished working paper) defined an inventory of wetlands listing 28 sites of international importance, and 64 sites of national or regional importance; the Institut Européen d'Ecologie (1981) provided an inventory of French bogs; Fournier et al. (1979) published a report on French wetlands of importance for Anatidae, which gathers data on 26 large wetlands; Scott (1980) listed 42 wetlands of international importance for waterfowl; and Marion (1982), within the framework of an inventory of sites of importance for the protection of birds in the EEC, established a list of French wetlands deserving special protection. This well-documented list categorizes approximately one hundred wetlands as requiring strict protection.

Several reports giving a general analysis of French wetlands also now exist. Mustin (1984) provides a qualitative survey by reviewing typical situations and major wetland problems, region by region. In addition to statistics, this report (unfortunately not published) gives a vivid picture of French wetland problems.

Several regions – for example Aquitaine, Alsace, Bretagne – have also produced their own inventory of regional wetland inventories, for use as tools in policy development or implementation.

## Major wetland types

Several major *inland freshwater marshes* are located on continental plains. Historically, these areas were often transformed into fishponds, where ponds, marshes, and wet farm and forest lands co-exist in a patchwork of high environmental interest. The biggest and most valuable such areas are: Sologne, Brenne, Dombes, and Etangs de Lorraine, but many smaller areas with similar attributes also exist.

Extensive agricultural development has left relatively few natural freshwater marshlands. Although generally not very numerous or large, these natural areas can be of significant environmental interest. Many of them are just small portions of broader "wet" areas, such as fishponds, or floodable meadows.

In lowland areas, there are relatively few residual *bogs*, but some of those that do persist have a very high environmental value. Most bogs are located in mountain regions – Alps, Jura, Vosges, Pyrénées, Massif Central – where they are by far the most frequent and environmentally important wetland type. However, they do not generally form large continuous areas, as they often do in more northern European countries.

There are no large areas of either *shrub or wooded swamps*. Occasionally, abandoned wet pastures are covered by shrubby vegetation, but these eventually end up being either wooded or flooded. There are some wet areas covered by forests, corresponding either to temporarily flooded zones; to wooded bogs; or to wet patches in "normal" forest stands. In other words, these areas are often wooded sections of larger wetland systems. Riparian forests, such as those along the Rhine, are very valuable, so the management of wooded swamps is quite important.

*Wet meadows, bottomlands and other riparian habitats* are very numerous, and often of high environmental importance. Two types of sub-areas exist in this category. The first includes large floodplain areas. Although most French rivers have already been modified, the floodplains of several large rivers, as well as some large areas of floodable lowlands, still retain part of their original characteristics. Significant river floodplains include the Loire, the Rhine (the wetland area is the Ried, in Alsace), the Saône, and the Adour. Large floodable lowlands of high environmental value include the freshwater part of the Marais de l'Ouest, in the western part of France; the best known of these is the Marais Poitevin.

A second category includes the many smaller, but much more numerous, floodplains and lowlands. The scale difference between these and their larger cousins makes them very different both in ecological terms, and in terms of environmental management problems. Less spectacular environmentally, more difficult to visualize when discussing national wetland problems, these areas still perform important environmental functions.

*Coastal saltmarsh* areas are large and environmentally important. It is relevant to distinguish between Atlantic coastal and Mediterranean marshes. Both are very different in many respects. Each coastal marsh, whether it be Atlantic or Mediterranean, is a fairly large functional system, with a variety of wetland habitats: natural seaside flats (tidal for the Atlantic); lagoons; artificial saltmarshes or salted fishponds; and a hinterland of freshwater lowlands. The major coastal wetlands include:

- the Atlantic: the Baie de Somme; the Mont St Michel; the Loire Estuary area; the Marais de l'Ouest (which includes a whole series of coastal wetlands on the west coast), and the Baie d'Arcachon;
- the Mediterranean: the Camargue; and a chain of lagoons more to the West in Languedoc.

Most *tidal freshwater wetlands* are used for aquaculture, and include some type of sea-defence work. Thus, tidal freshwater marshes are only marginal habitats, lying between the freshwater lowlands, and the salted coastal wetland. These habitats are usually treated as elements of the wider coastal wetland systems.

In short, French wetlands tend to fall under one of the following headings:

- large fishpond areas;
- residual freshwater marshes;
- scattered bogs;
- the floodplains of some large rivers;
- large freshwater farmed lowlands;
- smaller floodplains and lowlands;
- coastal wetlands (Atlantic);
- coastal wetlands (Mediterranean).

These categories reflect not only the different types of wetlands that exist in France, they also reflect the different management problems and approaches that have grown up in the country over the years.

## Functions of wetlands

The capacity of wetlands to *remove nitrates and organic loads* from surface water is widely recognized. This capacity can be exploited either by the natural environment, or artificially, to meet human needs.

In France, there are some examples of artificial sewage treatment ponds, but the use of wetlands for artificial recycling is not widespread. A group of experts recently concluded that there is virtually no future in France for the use of natural wetlands as water purification areas. This is either because the available wetlands areas are too limited; or because their ecological value is too high for it to be acceptable to use them for purification.

On the other hand, riparian wetlands have been shown to play a key role in the natural removal of nitrates from surface aquifers. (This relationship has been proven recently in the Garonne basin.) Similarly, the role of some coastal wetlands in purifying bay waters, and the natural role of some wetlands in purifying water coming out of drainage systems have both been demonstrated in specific locations. However, there has been no work done on the economic value of these purification functions; nor are they traditionally recognized as a factor to be taken into account in management planning. Nevertheless, the important role of coastal wetlands in bay water quality is now becoming better recognized, especially by aquacultural interests.

The *groundwater storage and recharge* function of wetlands has also been proven to exist, at least in some areas. Beyond the fact that the protection of water catchment areas can occasionally also apply to wetlands, the specific role of wetlands in aquifer recharge or storage does not seem to have often been considered when decisions affecting the natural environment have been made.

The ability of wetlands to *delay or to buffer floods* is officially acknowledged in France only reluctantly. For example, the official position of the Ministry of Agriculture is that land drainage has no negative effects on the flood regimes of drained watersheds. The flood-buffering capacity is hardly ever interpreted as a positive attribute of wetlands. More typically, it is taken as a sign of insufficient river works.

In other words, the fact that an area is occasionally flooded is usually considered to be an engineering *problem*, rather than an environmental *solution*. Similarly, the argument that letting an area flood periodically can help economize on costly flood-protection works tends, in the French decision system, to be interpreted as an indication that budgets for engineering works are too low, and should be increased.

The contribution of organic matter to the sea via coastal wetlands, that is, *food-web support*, has been shown to exist in the USA. Recent French studies indicate that a reverse process may be occurring: that is, that wetlands trap organic matter from the sea. This role of coastal wetlands as a "sink" for organic matter is positive, in that it helps to limit the organic content and risk of eutrophication in adjacent coastal areas – for instance, in the Baie du Mont St Michel.

The role of wetlands as a wildlife habitat is a widely-acknowledged and prominent function of French wetlands. It is also a primary argument in favour of their protection.However, no precise economic valuation of this function yet exists, so questions about how much protection is enough still persist.

A wide variety of *commercial outputs* are also derived from French wetlands. Poplar plantations cover approximately two hundred thousand hectares, for a total production of about one and half million cubic metres per year. Aquaculture is a significant activity in all fishpond areas and for significant areas of coastal wetlands, many of which include wetlands of very high environmental value. Low-intensity grazing plays a big role in the management of floodplains and lowlands, and of grasslands in general. However, it is difficult to determine what portion of total cattle/dairy production can be attributed specifically to wet grasslands. Many other production activities exist, including peat (not so much for fuel as for horticulture); reed and other helophytes, which are rather marginal activities in the aggregate, even if they may play a locally significant role.

Hunting is probably the most important of all *recreational uses* of French wetlands. Waterfowl – both resident and migratory – is the basis of this active economic sector. Hunting interests also exercise significant political and administrative influence over wetland management.

Apart from hunting, most recreational uses are linked to local circumstances, such as proximity to tourist bases, or, to local wetlands with unique landscape or wildlife values. The more general recreational activities are usually based on some direct interest in the natural environment, such as birdwatching, botany, and photography. These activities are much less developed in France than they are in some other countries, such as the United Kingdom and the United States.

France has several wetlands – such as the Camargue, the Lac de Grandlieu, the Baie d'Arcachon and others – which are clearly worth conserving for their ecologic and aesthetic merits. In practical terms, *aesthetic values* are often poorly recognized by the general public and by decision-makers. As a result, there is a direct link between public education and communication about wetlands on the one hand, and recognition of the "intrinsic" values of wetlands, on the other.

Wetlands also serve broader environmental functions than those described above. There are two main perspectives from which to assess the importance of these functions which are:

(i) the importance of wetlands in the overall environmental problem in France; and
(ii) the importance of French wetlands in the global management of European wetlands.

With regard to the former, it is only relatively recently that wetlands have started to emerge as a major theme in French environmental policies. In the early 1980s (and especially between 1982 and 1985), there was an explosion of studies and other initiatives that promoted wetlands to a leading position on the French governmental agenda. This trend was not especially French. In fact, it seems to have been the consequence of a much wider growth of interest in wetlands as a dominant environmental theme at the international level. In attempting to explain this sudden emergence of interest on wetlands, two factors ought to be underlined. The first is the fact that individual wetlands had long been recognized as sites of high environmental interest, and as such, had been studied and/or protected. But each such site tended to be considered for its own fauna, flora, or landscape values. The recent trend has been to attempt to "federate" many local and diverse situations under the heading "wetlands" – in effect to make them add up to a major "wetland" problem, to allow them to be dealt with at a higher level of decision-making.

The second factor is that most French wetlands are not wilderness areas at all, but are part of the rural fabric. The first wave of Nature Protection policies, especially the National Parks, had singled out for special protection those sites which were largely outside the economic system: mountains; rocky coasts; singular spots of nature and landscape; and so on. In the 1970s, however, the focus of interest in ecological parameters (flora, fauna, landscape) moved closer and closer to the fronts of economic development. Since many ecologically-interesting sites are also wetlands, more and more local situations were brought to the attention of environmental policies, until they were eventually "federated" under the generic term "wetlands".

The importance of French wetlands in the context of European wetlands is harder to evaluate. There are individual French wetlands areas of undebatable international interest, for example the Camargue; the Baie de l'Aiguillon; the Baie du Mont St Michel; and others. The preliminary inventory of wetlands of international importance for waterfowl in western Europe and northwest Africa mentions 42 such wetlands in France (compared with 114 for the UK; 49 for the Netherlands; 49 for Italy; and seven for Belgium). This data suggests that French wetlands have an average position in terms of their international importance. However, this is an incomplete view, and may very well be inaccurate. In the absence of more comparative data, it is sufficient to note here that the number and size of French wetlands, their variety, their geographic position on important migratory routes, all indicate that French wetlands play a significant role in the health of European, and even global, wetland stocks.

In summary, French wetland policies vary with: (i) the physical characteristics of wetlands; and (ii) what values are placed on these functions.

The natural attributes of French wetlands are now relatively well-recognized, after several years of intense effort by environmental actors to gain this recognition. In particular, habitat functions for waterfowl hunting; for birdlife; for fishing; and for interesting fauna and flora are relatively well-understood by the general public. The potential role of wetlands in water quality processes is currently the subject of significant research, and may eventually make its way into the technical considerations that lead to decisions either to transform or to conserve wetlands.

In contrast, the ecosystem values of wetlands (for example, their role in water management), and therefore, much of their inherent economic value, are much less widely recognized. Three basic reasons seem to explain this phenomenon:

(i) geographic characteristics, in particular the smaller unit size of many wetland types (e.g. bogs), and the high degree of artificialization of the French landscape make it difficult to gain public recognition in France for the idea of wetlands as a "total" resource that requires conservation;
(ii) the concept of integrating the needs of natural systems into economic planning and project design is still not widespread among French engineers; and
(iii) the economic values of wetlands as a resource comprise only a very limited percentage of the public interest in France, compared, for example, with the pressures of special-interest groups (hunters, environmentalists, farmers).

The latter two problems make it difficult for a full consideration of the economic values of the natural wetland environment to emerge in France. Wetland management tends to develop into a polarized debate between those who recognize their environmental value, and those who would rather not have wetlands at all. As a result, economic actors who want to use wetland resources as part of their productive processes, such as estuarine fishermen; farmers with low productivity cattle raising systems; and so on, become marginalized. Hunters are a special case. Their activity is quite important economically, but their interests are defended largely in political, rather than in economic, terms. For all practical purposes, the powerful hunting lobby is engaged in defending the *environmental values* of wetlands. As a result, *economic values* of wetlands are either residual or virtual (that is, associated with development projects which are not actually implemented). Later sections of this chapter develop these topics further. The important conclusion here is that, in France, wetlands are perceived almost entirely in environmental terms, rather than in economic ones.

## French wetlands under threat

The dominant threats will be quite different, depending usually on the type of wetland involved. It is, therefore, at the level of wetland types that it seems most appropriate to discuss threats to wetlands.

The large fishpond areas are caught between two symmetrical types of threat. The first of these is the gradual abandonment of traditional fish-farming and farming practices. When this abandonment leads to a discontinuation in the management of these areas, the result is an environmental loss, and a much greater vulnerability to projects that might radically alter them. The second threat is the modernization of freshwater fish-farming techniques, when these techniques are implemented without proper environmental concern and design. This leads to the loss of many desirable environmental qualities of these areas in terms of flora, fauna, and landscapes.

Valuable "residual" marshes and bogs are often exposed, because of their small size, to a great number of threats, such as agricultural drainage, hydrological disruption, filling and dredging, public works, or urbanization. However, because of the concentration of their environmental values on small surfaces, and because of their limited economic use, this type of resource is also much more likely than other wetlands to be protected by a variety of rather well-developed tools, such as nature reserves, and "arrêtés de biotopes". Once they are protected, or even when they are simply not threatened, the problem of how they are managed also becomes important.

The floodplains of large rivers are under significant threat from hydraulic works for flood control, drainage or energy production. Historic and current losses in this category in France are considerable. The potential for future losses likely to occur because of projects presently under discussion is also significant. Hard data does not exist in this area, because a systematic survey has not yet been undertaken, and would be extremely difficult to carry out, for a variety of reasons. In particular, it would be hard to decide when a floodable wetland ceases to be a wetland. Since it is all a matter of degree, it would be difficult to judge the point at which change actually takes place. What can be done, however, is to inventory major losses that have occurred in the past and to predict changes likely to occur in the near future. This work has not been done in a systematic fashion, but prominent examples include:

- *for the recent past*: the Redon marshes (Brittany), and the Lônes of Bregnier-Cordon (upper Rhône Valley);
- *for the near future*: the Loire River, the Saône, and the Garonne.

Both floodplains and farmed freshwater lowlands are regularly converted into arable land via drainage projects. Agriculture drainage continues to be an important element of public-sector policy, despite appearances to the contrary. Because of administrative and political "decentralization" in 1982, funds for these projects are no longer administered in Paris. Consequently, there is no official drainage enhancement policy at the national level. However, the programmes which were previously funded at the national level are now being actively continued on the regional scale, funded both by the "régions" and by the "départements". The works are often administered and planned, as before, by the regional services of the Ministry of Agriculture. The result is that large drainage projects are underway, or are being planned for implementation during the next five years, in areas of major environmental value. In some regions, for example Pays de la Loire, public funding for drainage in environmentally-sensitive areas will be higher in the next five years than it has been in the past twenty years.

Several smaller lowlands and floodplains are also threatened by drainage projects and riverworks, with correspondingly lower public visibilities. These projects also suffer from problems which affect larger wetlands, such as dredging and filling, road construction and afforestation.

With regard to coastal wetlands, several threats have to be considered. Their freshwater components are mainly damaged by agricultural drainage and reclamation. The artificial saltmarshes and the salt fishponds, which cover large surfaces of great environmental value, are often threatened by the discontinuation of the economic practices that helped to promote their conservation, such as salt production and low-yield fish-farming. Symmetrically, modern (intensive) aquacultural practices are creating an increasing threat to coastal wetlands. Urbanization, public works, and roads, also take a high toll on coastal wetlands. On the coast, the economic pressure for space, especially space considered to be of marginal economic value, such as wetlands, is very high.

In general, it seems appropriate to conclude that French wetlands suffer:

- from general threats which tend to erode all types of natural environments, such as urbanization, roadworks and other infrastructure;
- from two other types of threats more specific to wetlands: agricultural drainage, and hydraulic works on rivers; and
- from a more insidious problem: the gradual disappearance of the economic practices which have historically helped to maintain the environmental values of many French wetlands.

On the whole, agriculture appears to be the major single cause of wetland degradation in France. Of 34 sites in Brittany, for instance, 14 were damaged by drainage and conversion to arable or intensive pasture; 9 were filled; 3 were damaged by roads; 3 more by urbanization; 2 by camping sites; and 1 each was damaged by chronic pollution, construction of a sewage treatment station and construction of a sports ground. It is probable that figures would show an even stronger role of agriculture in a case study focusing specifically on inland wetlands. A similar dominance of agricultural threats is visible in larger wetlands.

## Market and intervention failure

As emphasized above, the main threats to wetlands in France come from agricultural drainage, or from river hydraulics projects. It is very difficult to think of even one example in France of such a project where market variables would not be strongly overshadowed by interventions by government and other public bodies.

In the case of agriculture, variables crucial to a farmer's economic decisions – about product prices; tax burdens on the land; price of inputs, such as water for irrigation, interest rates on loans for farming equipment, and so on – are so influenced by public policies (both national and European), that it is no longer possible to imagine how market forces might operate without this intervention. In the specific case of wetlands, there are very few examples where farmers make wetland management decisions (like drainage) without some type of intervention from government bodies – through direct subsidies, technical advice, tax breaks, exceptional interest rates, and so on.

In France, farmers co-operate with public bodies to ensure the long-term viability of the farm. Part of this viability requires a certain income for the farmer – typically negotiated through the unions, in terms of the price of products, social help available, and so on. Thus, there is no clear-cut separation between the (private) economic operator and the (public) regulator. Public bodies and farmers see themselves as running an important economic sector together. This co-operation is very close at the precise level where wetland management decisions are made: drainage works, choice of production levels, and choice of techniques. In brief, market and intervention policies are closely intertwined in France. However, at the level of important wetland management decisions, public intervention is the crucial element.

Looking at the second major threat to wetlands (that is hydraulic works on rivers), we reach a similar conclusion. River works are typically undertaken either by public bodies or by publicly-owned corporations. Previous case studies have shown that the decisions to undertake such works are very insensitive to economic (for example cost-benefit) evaluations. Clearly, public-intervention policy, rather than market forces, predominates here as well.

The "externalities" caused by agricultural or river "improvement" projects, are also significant. Again, these effects are mitigated largely by public intervention, mainly through the arbitration of conflicts raised by actors suffering from the externalities, or through negotiations among public bodies which are defending different views of how wetlands should be managed. In these negotiations, as discussed below, the evaluation of economic consequences of projects once again plays a rather minor role.

## *Market failure*

As a result, it is very difficult to directly apply the concept of market failure to the destruction and degradation of French wetlands. Only very seldom is the degradation of a wetland the result of an economic choice by an independent owner in a market, even an imperfect market. If one excludes wetlands managed for "natural" uses (for example hunting protection), there are few wetlands, and only small ones at that, which belong to one owner. Decisions are made collectively, almost always under direct or indirect management by public organizations. Agricultural decisions are also taken in a context where the micro-economics of the choice are directly determined by public interventions. Furthermore, such decisions are often made in direct contradiction to what an economic assessment of the variables involved would suggest.

One area where market considerations might be separable from intervention policy in agriculture is in the organization of product markets. In particular, production quotas and "label" policies for quality products are part of this sub-set. Currently, the allocation of milk quotas is a major issue in the management of all marginal farmland areas, including wetlands. Favouring these areas in the geographic allocation of quotas within French regions would help provide more stable markets for production in pastured wetlands, thereby enhancing prospects for their conservation. However, such policies are naturally opposed by other farming interests. In some cases, it may be possible to promote the sustainable management of environmentally-important wetlands by giving their products a label indicating their specific qualities. This is the case, for instance, for the Mont St Michel area, which produces salted pasture mutton, considered to be of superior quality. However, the Mont St Michel label is not protected by regulation, meaning that the Mont St Michel price is closer to that of plain mutton. This makes it difficult for Mont St Michel farmers to sustain the costs of raising sheep under wetland conditions, and, consequently, threatens the long-term viability of the Mont St Michel wetlands.

## *Intervention failure*

It is appropriate to begin a discussion of intervention failures with an example of how public policies determine the day-to-day choices of farmers which affect the management of wetlands. To begin with, existing policies systematically prevent farmers from obtaining accurate information about the economic potential of wetlands used for pastures. Publicly-funded agronomic research does not seek technical solutions for the improvement of wet grasslands or marshes. Although present indications are that a higher economic potential could be realized for many of these lands, virtually all research effort is focused on techniques for drainage and conversion to arable land. Technical advice is, therefore, widely available to farmers, but only for the objective of intensifying agricultural activity through land drainage and conversion.

Secondly, all farmers share the cost of arterial drainage, whether they wish it or not. This imposes extra costs on those who might wish to develop a system based on lower cost regimes, for example regimes that are more "friendly" to wetlands.

The result of these distortions in the economics of farming on wetlands are self-fulfilling. Poor returns on wetland areas then justify further moves of agronomical research, farmer information, technical advice, and investment decisions, away from the rational use of wet pastures. This "wet pastures vicious circle" has been identified as one of the most significant factors inhibiting an environmentally sound and economically efficient use of French wetlands, especially in floodplains, pastured coastal wetlands, wet meadows and grazed peatlands.

In this "circle", public policies have an indirect negative impact on wetlands by placing farmers in highly-distorted market conditions. But public policies also play a more direct role in determining what will become of a wetland. This is the case, in particular, for major agricultural drainage projects, as well as for hydraulic and other public works. Two examples will illustrate the magnitude of this problem.

The first example is that of arterial drainage in the "Marais de l'Ouest". Major drainage projects already underway in this region have a serious impact on large areas of wet meadows with a high environmental significance. Some of the interventions which lead to such a negative result are:

- farmers pay a land tax. However, wet meadows carry a much higher tax than very productive irrigated cornland nearby. When the tax rates were last revised at the turn of the century, wet meadows were much more productive than they are today. This land tax (in the order of FF 1000 per hectare per year) imposes a large handicap on any use of these lands compatible with their limitations. The Ministry of Finance, supported by the farmers of the lower tax areas, has been vigorously opposed to any revision to the tax regime, for obvious reasons;
- existing research and training policies work against the improvement of wet pastures (as previously explained);
- drainage is undertaken collectively, and is highly subsidized. This creates an artificial bonus for conversion, and a penalty on the economic use of wet meadows for pastures;
- farm products (especially cereals) are often bought at prices which do not reflect market conditions; and
- the Corps of Engineers serves either as decision-maker or as a technical adviser to local authorities on all decisions affecting drainage projects. However, the Corps also receives a commission on drainage works that it constructs. The resulting reserves are used to complement the salaries of engineers and technicians who make the decisions, and who carry out the works. This system constitutes a substantial incentive to advise or decide in favour of more engineering works, and to ignore opportunities for other possible uses of public money.

The second example comes from careful *ex poste* studies of economic evaluations which had led to implementation of projects damaging wetlands. Two hydro-power dams have been studied in this way. The first was built on the Rhône river, and damaged riparian wetlands of high ecological interest. The second one was built in the Alps, drowning a mountain wetland of high landscape and ecological value. In both cases, careful review of the sophisticated cost-benefit studies presented by the utility for the public inquiries, and the subsequent authorization procedures, proved that the original economic evaluation had been biased. In one case, the final cost of construction ended up being 60 per cent higher than planned. In another case, parameters entering into the original evaluation had been biased in the first phase, in order to generate artificially high expected rates of return, and thus to obtain a permit for the dam. These parameters had then been biased once again in subsequent negotiations in order to help the utility obtain a low minimum water flow for the natural bed of the river.

Another similar example comes from the closing of the Vilaine River estuary. A study sponsored by the National Hunting Bureau (1983) shows that hydraulic works which have had a very serious environmental effect on wetlands have cost FF 15 000 per hectare, with minimal improvements in production. The current price of the land, even after the works, is still only FF 5000 to 7000. If the damage caused by the works to shellfish production in the estuary was also taken into account, the original economic evaluation clearly ought to have been negative.

These case studies and others support the conclusion that, in the French decision-making process, economic evaluations play a relatively insignificant role. The achievement of long-term technical programmes, and the ability of various public bodies to secure sufficient budget allocations are far more critical to the ultimate impacts on wetlands. As Claude Henry has shown in a study (Henry, personal communication, 1989) of decision-making processes in public works in France, the Netherlands and England, the French situation is characterized by a high level of commitment to ambitious, long-term technical programmes, for example aerospace technology, Concorde, or nuclear energy. This is especially the case for agricultural drainage programmes, and for hydraulic works on rivers, two areas of public intervention which have a very high impact on wetlands. These programmes are endowed with such financial means and decision-making power that it is very difficult for lower priority objectives, such as financial return on public expenditure, or environmental conservation, to receive a fair treatment in the decision-making process.

In a wider sense, it is not always clear whether the set of intervention policies that lead to the environmental degradation of wetlands should be considered an intervention "failure". Indeed, the concept of intervention failure suggests that there is some intention to manage wetlands with environmental objectives in mind in the first place; and that the measures taken to do so do not lead to the desired results.

Public bodies responsible for interventions affecting wetlands typically have no explicit wetland objectives in mind when developing or implementing their interventions. Therefore, all arguments regarding the values of wetlands; the importance of managing them as public goods; and the problems raised by the irreversibility of their loss have to be put forward by the actors of environmental policy. This group essentially includes the Ministry of Environment; its local services, and the bodies affiliated with it; the Nature Protection Association; and environmental specialists in various non-governmental organizations.

Recent attention given to the problems of wetlands has not yet resulted in the adoption of specific wetland policies. It is only through the general procedures of environmental management – impact studies; "declaration d'utilité publique"; public inquiries; and so on – that the value of wetlands is introduced into public choices on projects affecting wetlands. In recent years (roughly since 1982), wetlands have moved up very quickly on the public environmental agenda. Wetlands are no longer totally neglected as an environmental problem, as they once were.

In contrast, wetlands have made very little progress, over the same time period, up the priority list of those public bodies responsible for the policies that physically affect wetlands. If French public policies, especially in the fields of agriculture and public works, tend to result in the degradation of wetlands, it is essentially because of the failure of attempts to co-ordinate efforts between the various administrations involved, and the failure to include wetland management objectives specifically into those policies which affect wetlands. In other words, the problem is not that interventions fail to achieve their wetland management objectives, but that environmental policies and government co-ordination fail to introduce wetland management objectives into the agendas of operational ministries and agencies in the first place.

## *Significance of market and intervention failures*

Evaluating the damages inflicted on wetlands by economic market behaviour and by public sector policies that do not take wetlands into account, is very difficult at a global level. The main reasons for this difficulty are:

- the heterogeneity of wetlands, both in that many different types exist, and in their condition at the start of any given period;
- the absence of a global inventory of French wetlands;
- the fact that in large wetlands, damage is always relative (functional), and thus hard to express in terms of physical areas that have been lost; and
- the difficulty of evaluating how a wetland which is heavily dependent on human intervention would evolve if it were not submitted to a given development project (the "baseline scenario estimation" problem).

Although it would thus be adventurous to attempt a quantitative assessment of damages in this case study, numerous indications exist to the seriousness of the degradation of wetlands in France. The National Hunting Bureau, for instance (ONC, 1981), has singled out 25 French wetlands as being of major importance for waterfowl. Of these, 13 are currently being damaged by drainage projects. Nine more are judged to be vulnerable to such projects if current policies are continued. Since there is no evidence that known trends in drainage programmes have changed since this assessment was done, or that they will change in the near future, this rough data points to the conclusion that French wetlands are still undergoing serious damage.

Another approach to evaluating the significance of the damage inflicted on wetlands is to look at major losses in the near past, or losses expected for the near future. Examples abound:

- wetlands recently destroyed by drainage or submersion (including Marais des Echets; Marais de St Gond; communal marsh of Vouillé; Fecht valley; and so on);
- wetlands currently undergoing rapid destruction (Ried

d'Alsace, Marais de Lavours; Brittany bogs; the Loire estuary; riparian forest along the Rhine, and so on); and

- wetlands threatened by projects presently under discussion, (including the Loire valley; coastal marshes around the Loire Estuary; the valley of the Saône).

A third perspective on damages undergone by French wetlands is obtained by following the current activities of institutions in charge of wetland protection in the various *régions* or *départements*. Virtually all of these institutions are now watching projects that would affect significant wetland areas, should they be implemented.

There are some signs that wetlands are more often taken into account in the decision-making process now than in the past. But the conclusion is inescapable that both major projects and gradual deterioration through pollution or encroachment continue to take a high toll on French wetlands every year.

## Economic valuation of wetlands

In the early 1980s, the French Ministry of the Environment launched several studies designed to assess the possibility of evaluating more precisely the costs of environmental damage in economic terms. The initial hope of the programme was that economic valuation of these damages would help to integrate environmental considerations into the decision-making processes leading to large development projects.

The first findings of this programme indicated that, although methodologies for the economic valuation of environmental goods had been available in the 1970s, these methods seemed to have been little used in France. Further inquiries confirmed that impression. This led to a series of case studies of decision-making processes, aimed at suggesting ways of improving the process. The case studies included hydro-power dams; highway construction; a toxic waste dump; a wetland drainage scheme; and industrial harbour development projects. Somewhat to the surprise of the researchers, it was found that (as previously discussed) in none of the cases, did economic calculations play an important role in decision-making. Approval for all of the projects had been given when large long-term technical needs coincided with political and budgetary support. Moreover, if the economic studies backing the projects had been carefully screened at the time, none of them would have passed the test. Of all projects, the one with the *least* defensible economic parameters was the wetland drainage project. This project has since been largely implemented.

In effect, it is apparent that most of the projects which severely affect French wetlands would not pass "muster" on their economic merits alone, even without taking into account the economic cost of their impact on wetlands. This observation can lead to either of two seemingly-opposite practical conclusions:

(i) that the economic value of their impacts on wetlands should be systematically added to other economic evidence, in order to justify rejection of some projects which have insufficient economic/ecological merits; or

(ii) that, since projects affecting wetlands are not decided on economic terms anyway, it is not very useful to argue in favour of introducing of the economic valuations of wetlands into the decision-making process.

On closer reflection, however, these two conclusions may not be incompatible. Taken together, they suggest that a dual approach to the economics of wetland management in the French context may be appropriate.

Based on existing evidence that calculated economic analyses carry little weight with decision-makers, it seems appropriate to base wetland conservation strategies on the process as it now exists. This means that policies which address:

- the technical culture of engineers;
- the availability (as perceived by local decision-makers) of alternative types of development projects which incorporate wetland values; and
- opportunities for continued pressure on the decision-making process through the existing tools of environmental policy.

But evidence also suggests that a more careful consideration of the "real" economics of proposed projects would be beneficial, both from an economic and an environmental point of view. In combination with the policy approach suggested above, which starts from how decision-making systems affecting wetland management actually work, it would also be advisable to press for a gradual change of these systems towards a better use of economic evaluation tools.

In fact, these conclusions are consistent with the two major current trends in French wetlands management policy:

(i) the inclusion of wetlands as a major theme for action by environmental lobbies and administrations; and
(ii) the search for technical and economic solutions for the sustainable use of wetlands.

## The place of wetlands in general environmental policies

Once the environmental importance of wetlands is admitted, two ways of promoting their sound management are possible. The first is to have explicit inclusion of wetlands in existing environmental policies. The second is to create a separate wetland management policy. In the case of France, an almost exclusive choice has been made for the former approach. A review of the range of instruments available for wetland management policy in France would coincide strictly with a description of French environmental policy instruments in general:

- planning designations;
- impact studies and public inquiries for projects;
- nature reserves, national parks, regional parks;
- protection of species;
- acquisition (Conservatoire du Littoral);
- adaptation of development policies to environmentally sensitive areas.

Although wetlands have recently risen to a much higher position on the environmental agenda, no specific wetland policy yet exists. What are the reasons for this decision, and how should its effects be evaluated?

The review of functions of wetlands in France – both those

which actually exist, as well as those which are recognized as such – has shown that the majority of the stress occurs on wetlands which are habitats for flora or fauna (especially wildfowl), and as biotopes of special interest. For this reason, wetlands have become a high priority in nature conservation policies. There is no particular need for specific wetlands policies to protect these functions, since they are typically taken care of through the general nature conservation policies.

We have also seen that only a very small percentage of French wetlands remain in their original state, and that wetlands are very much a part of the rural fabric of the country. In countries with low population densities and a low level of wetland artificialization, it is conceivable to approach the management of wetlands in a "statistical" manner. In these situations, one begins by making an inventory of wetlands of a certain type. One can then choose rationally how many of these wetlands can be "sacrificed" to development, and under what specific environmental and economic criteria. The result is the formulation of "wetland policy" in these countries. However, this approach does not seem well-suited to the French situation. Each individual case in France is unique, both in terms of the *economic* actors (because they usually have no alternative locations available), and in terms of the *environmental* actors (because they are typically attempting to conserve only one of a very small number of wetlands).

Another aspect of this situation is that wetland problems in France are usually dealt with in a highly adversarial context. Each case is fought directly on its political-economic merits, as well as on its environmental merits. The debate is filtered through a decision-making process that is highly dependent on the strategies of the actors involved. For a given wetland policy to be possible to implement it has to be designed, or at least agreed upon, by the institution responsible for development projects, in particular, by the Ministry of Agriculture, as well as by those in charge of the environment. Between 1982 and 1986, an evolution towards the better integration of wetland management into the policies of the Ministry of Agriculture was occurring. Signs of this progress included a Convention between the Ministries of Environment and Agriculture, as well as several joint pilot projects. However, for the last three years, this trend has been reversed, and wetland problems are again being treated on a more adversarial basis.

It is worth underlining that the French Ministry of Agriculture has no official definition of wetlands. The only concept used is that of "terres humides", which include both arable land with an excess of water in soils, and wetlands in the sense used by environmental agencies. The Ministry has consistently refused to develop any mechanism that would create a systematic differentiation between projects affecting wetlands and those affecting other drainage projects. As one official put it: "the Ministry is prepared to take wetland problems into account only in cases where they are raised by opponents stridently enough, and with enough strategic cunning to make us have to take them into account".

Overall, there is no reason to expect that wetland management should do any better in France than environmental management in general; and wetlands have reached a fairly high priority within environmental policies, so there is little apparent need for a specific wetland policy.

Instead, wetlands are just another example of the need for better integration of environmental concerns into economic development policies, which is, in itself, a fairly difficult task. In other words, the fact that it is appropriate for wetland policy in France to be considered a part of general environmental policies does not diminish the necessity of allowing wetland management objectives to penetrate decision-making in economic sectors affecting wetland management. Wetland issues have taken the first step in climbing to a relatively high position on the French environmental agenda. The priorities should now be to establish efficient dialogue and co-ordination between public bodies in charge of the environment, and their counterparts in the economic sectors.

Up to this point, the discussion has focused mostly on those values of wetlands associated with hunting – recreation and nature conservation – which are dominant in the French context. But it is also worthwhile considering their water quality functions, in particular the role that wetlands play on littoral water quality. Using the preceding analysis, a reasonable approach would be to integrate wetland management considerations into the policies of the institutions responsible for water quality. However, this has not traditionally been the case in France. As far as fresh water is concerned, the organizations concerned again have a bias towards hydraulic engineering. There is little room in this approach for ambitious efforts to influence the use of wetlands which, because of the way administrative boundaries are established, can escape direct responsibility. For coastal waters, the problem is even more difficult, because co-ordination between maritime authorities and those in charge of the land areas where wetlands are located is very difficult to achieve.

In summary, wetlands conservation and management already receive an adequate proportion of the emphasis within French environmental management policies; the poor integration of environmental policies in general into development policies is a major obstacle to improvements in the conservation and management of French wetlands; and wetland management should receive more attention in the framework of public policies oriented towards water quality and in the management of resources based on water quality.

## The search for environmentally appropriate economic development

So far, this chapter has indicated that French wetlands suffer much environmental damage from development projects. These projects often cannot be justified on either economic or (at least for agricultural projects) technical grounds. What are the reasons for this?

One reason is the "wet pastures vicious circle". As already discussed, this phenomenon causes agricultural research and development to be biased against the development of wetlands in a way that satisfies environmental objectives. This bias in agricultural policies is probably the single most important negative factor in the evolution of French wetlands policy. Mustin describes the cycle leading to the destruction of coastal Mediterranean wetlands in the following way.

> As observed elsewhere, like in Brittany, the threats start with:
>
> - the disappearance of the traditional uses of the wetland (horse or cattle raising, fishing, and so on);

- the appearance of wasteland, rapidly drying up, and sometimes used as refuse dumps;
- the intervention of local authorities to improve this degraded situation leads them to make irreversible decisions, through filling; the transition to a terrestrial habitat, and so on.

The disappearance of the wetland is only the conclusion of a more or less protracted evolution, which starts as soon as the ecosystem is no longer managed in its historical vocation of producing natural and agricultural resources.

(Mustin, 1984)

The need for environmentally-sound economic development of wetlands has both ecological and socio-economic roots. From an ecological perspective, French wetlands depend so much on artificial hydraulic systems, and on management of the local vegetation, that they have to be actively managed if they are to retain their environmental value. From a socio-economic perspective, it is politically impossible for government administrators to avoid new development initiatives for regions which have significant economic problems. They will tend to prefer any project, even if it is not economically or environmentally viable, to no project at all. Only the presence or absence of tangible, locally available, alternatives to these projects will be actively considered.

Another aspect of the same problem is the management of protected wetland areas. It is not enough to shield a wetland from external economic pressures to ensure its conservation. Several examples have shown the French environmental community that protected wetland sites require intensive management, usually with very limited funds. One of the best known cases is that of the natural reserve of Mannevilles, in the Marais Vernier. In this pilot project, the regional park has illustrated that the introduction of Highland Cattle provided an efficient way of managing a wetland economically, at the same time improving its environmental value.

Consequently, the development of economically viable and environmentally appropriate uses for various types of wetlands is necessary:

- to prevent the long-term evolution of a wetland to the point where an environmentally damaging project will be unavoidable;

- as alternatives to environmentally inappropriate development projects;
- as solutions for the long-term management of protected wetlands; and
- as a common ground between the organizations in charge of wetland conservation and those in charge of development projects.

In 1985 and 1986, the CESTA led a working group, gathering scientific experts from the Ministries of Agriculture and Environment, and from research institutes studying the use of wetlands. The group reviewed existing innovative French experiments in the use and management of wetlands, inviting the individual experts who had promoted these projects. The experiences gained were evaluated on the basis of several criteria:

- technical success and reliability, current and potential;
- economic performance, both current and potential;
- environmental soundness, both currently and under various assumptions about environmental vigilance or further economic evolution;
- replicability in other sites; and
- the types and areas of wetland that could be affected by the technology.

The review showed that for all types of wetlands, there were several promising possibilities for development projects that were sounder than existing ones, both on economic and environmental grounds. However, it was also concluded that such techniques would require much more effort and testing, if they were to be applied more widely than just under test conditions. More specifically, the group concluded that:

(i) research and development in the field of improving, *without drainage*, wet pastures was a priority, in view of both the large areas of wetlands directly dependent on these activities and on the basis of promising technical-economical conditions;
(ii) the cropping of helophytes and the use of wood from wetland trees could both be improved, and applied to

larger areas than at present;

(iii) technical developments in freshwater pond fish-farming indicate potential for the better use of ponds, but that these methods could also present high risks if they were not submitted to close environmental scrutiny. These methods had already resulted in the transformation of some ponds into basins (for example, via the suppression of reed-belts and muddy shores);

(iv) recent trends toward the use of artificial coastal wetlands for aquaculture were significant for the long-term protection of tourism-intensive coastal wetlands. Environmental concerns should be integrated early into the technical and economic development of such wetlands;

(v) the management of wetlands for hunting is a flourishing economic activity; and

(vi) French wetlands are generally ill-suited to the disposal of sewage. The positive effects of wetlands on water quality, and their management to take economic advantage of these effects, are the subject of significant ongoing research, but are still a long way from field applications.

## Economics and sustainable wetland management

Another conclusion of the group was of particular relevance for this chapter. This was that having techniques for the sound economic and environmental use of wetlands is *necessary*, but by no means *sufficient*, to ensure their conservation. In fact, in nearly all the examples studied, a strong possibility existed that wetland use might evolve towards more economically-intensive and less environmentally-satisfactory results. A few examples will illustrate this problem.

1 A farmer wishes to intensify the cultivation of his land. A careful mapping of the land reveals that part of it can be converted to arable use in a profitable way, and that another part (the most environmentally sensitive) would be too costly to convert. The farmer follows these findings, and his development project is cited as a good example of enhancing the sustainable use of natural resources. After some years, however, he has accumulated enough money

from the improved farming to allow him to cover the higher costs of draining the lower parts of his lands, and to make that conversion somewhat profitable through the economies of scale achieved by his (now largely amortized) equipment. So, conversion takes place. In this case, the original environmentally sound solution has been only an interim step towards the inevitable artificialization of the wetland.

2 Fish-farming is regarded as being useful to justify the maintenance of fishponds of high environmental value. Thus, farmers are helped by the Ministry of Agriculture, through an economic development programme that also satisfies environmental objectives. A new tool is then introduced onto the market, which allows farmers to cut reed-belts more efficiently. In a few years, most of the reed-belts in the pond area are gone. A decade ago, the wetlands were menaced by the discontinuation of fish-farming. Now, they are threatened by over-intensive fish-farming. This demonstrates the fragile balance between technology, economics, and environmental considerations on the road to sustainable development.

3 Hunting is a highly profitable economic use of wetlands in France – much more so than farming. For example, in the Somme, one hectare of hunting marshes sells at five times the price of nearby arable land, and is rented for between 20 and 50 times more revenue. Needless to say, there are not many examples of conversion of that land to agriculture! On the contrary, the temptation is high to buy even small plots of marsh for hunting purposes.There are several examples where such piecemeal acquisition of a marsh by individual hunters has led to paralysis in the management of the wider hydraulic system in which the marsh is located. This results in general environmental degradation, although the original purpose of the acquisition seemed quite compatible with protection of the wetland.

From these and other examples, the expert group concluded that aiming at the sustainable development of wetlands themselves is not sufficient. If wetlands are vulnerable to the decisions of one actor who functions from a purely economic perspective, seemingly "sustainable" techniques may only be the first step toward irreversible damage.

In other words, just as they are distinct "ecozones", at the crossroads of several ecological systems, wetlands are also often situated at the crossroads of different social uses and values. Although it is important to strive for their viable economic use, it is unlikely that maximizing the short-term profits of any one activity on wetlands will lead to a sustainable long-term result.

## Conclusions

This case study has illustrated the importance of wetland conservation and management for the French environment. For example, 86 per cent of the sites listed in the national inventory of Sites of Special Ecological, Faunistic or Floristic Significance are coastal or continental wetlands.

During the past ten years, as a result of numerous and sustained efforts, the conservation of wetlands has risen significantly in the priorities of the organizations responsible for environmental management in France.

However, this increased emphasis has also exposed large inadequacies in the integration of wetland considerations into the policies of organizations which are in charge of the projects damaging them most: agricultural drainage, hydraulic works on rivers, transportation, and urbanization.

In particular, the farming community and the Ministry of Agriculture both appear to be reluctant to give a special status to wetlands within the framework of their drainage programmes. This makes it impossible to assess – and even more difficult to control – the impact of a given policy on wetlands. The situation in this respect has deteriorated even further with recent decentralizations of the budgeting and expenditure authority for drainage projects. Wetland considerations find their way into the formal decision-making process only when a local conflict is brought to light by some environmental group, or when individual units within the Ministry of the Environment present objections to a given project.

The result of this type of intervention is that environmental questions are gradually obtaining greater public attention. As Mustin (1985) writes: "intensive corn cultivation projects, which would have been implemented despite regulations some years back, are now the object of strenuous triangular negotiations between government services, farming unions, and local governments". Depending on the specific case, such negotiations are apt to stop the project, to bring about a mitigation of its impacts, or to have no environmental results at all.

Nor do other government agencies responsible for projects with a major impact on wetlands typically have any particular wetland policy of their own. It is usually "project-by-project" management, on the basis of individual impact assessments. The result is that it is usually only quite late in the decision-making process that wetlands considerations are introduced.

Since wetlands form such a high proportion of the environmental impacts of certain development projects, for example drainage, and dam construction, it would be advisable to introduce special mechanisms to ensure that the public agencies in charge of such policies explicitly factor wetland constraints into their decisions.

Priority in further wetland initiatives in France should be given to:

- increased interaction between environmental and economic development administrations;
- more careful economic assessment of development projects affecting valuable wetlands;
- the introduction of environmentally sound wetland management competence, through education, professional training or incentives, into the design and planning practices of the organization(s) issuing development permits;
- further research and development on technologies for sustainable development of wetlands in various situations; and
- the inclusion of wetland management opportunities which could lead to improved water quality on the agendas of public agencies responsible for water quality.

## References

Baldock, D., *Wetland Drainage in Europe: the Effects of Agricultural Policy in four EEC Countries* (IIED-IEEP, 1984).

CEMAGREF, *Assainissement Agricole, Èconomie et Environnement Série des Études*, numéro 7 (1983).

CEMAGREF, *Impacts en Zones Humides* (1981).

CEMAGREF, *Les Fonctions Naturelles des Zones Humides* (1982).

Chantrel, C., *Eléments d'Étude pour un Bilan Économique de la Transformation des Azones Humides par l'Agriculture* (ONC, 1984).

Comité Interministériel de la Qualité de la Vie, *Communication "Agriculture-Environnement"* (1984).

EPA, *Les Hélophytes – Récolte et Valorisation des Végétaux Herbacés en Zone Humide* (ONC-Ministère de l'Agriculture, 1984).

Fournier, O. *et al.*, *Compte rendu du séminaire "Oiseaux d'Eau et Zones Humides"* (Paris: ONC, Section gibier d'eau, 1979).

Institut Européen d'Ecologie, *Inventaire des Tourbières de France* (Paris: Ministerè de l'Environnement, 1981).

Lebreton, P., *La Nature en Crise: Sang de la Terre* (1988).

Lecomte, T. *et al.*, "Restauration de Biocénoses Palustres par l'Utilisation d'une Race Bovine Ancienne: Cas de la Réserve des Mannevilles (Marais Vernier, Eure", *Bull. ecol.* (1981).

Marion, "Liste des Milieux à Protéger en France dans le Cadre de la Directive du Conseil de la CEE sur la Conservation des Oiseaux Sauvages" *Peun. Ar. Bed.*, vol. 13, pp.97–121 (1982).

Mayer, P., *Aménagement Aquacole des Marais Saumâres Endigués du Littoral et Planification Écologique* (CEMAGREF, 1984).

Mermet, D. and L. Mermet, *Bilan Économique de la Transformation des Milieux Humides par l'Agriculture: la mise en Culture d'un Marais – Économiquement Justifiée ou non? Une Étude de Cas dans le Marais Poitevin* (ONC, CESTA, 1983).

Mermet, L. and M. Mustin, *Assainissement Agricole et Régression des Zones Humides en France* (IEEP, 1983).

Mermet, L. (Ed.), *Terres et Eaux – Approches Techniques pour Conserver et Mettre en Valeur les Zones Humides* (CESTA, 1986).

Mermet, L., *Elaboration d'une Méthode d'Évaluation des Conséquences pour l'Environnement des Grands Projets d'Aménagement – Le Cas du Marais Poitevin* (SCORE, Laboratoire d'Econométrie de l'Ecole Polytechnique, 1982).

Ministry of the Environment, France, *The State of the Environment* (1985).

Mustin, M., *Les Zones Humides à Potentialités Fourragères, Valorisation Agronomique et Gestion Écologique* (ONC, 1985).

Mustin, M., *Réalisation d'un Fichier National sur les Zones Humides en Liaison avec les Grands Projets de Drainage et d'Aménagements Agricoles* (Hydro-M, Ministère de l'Environnement, 1984).

Office National de la Chasse, *Bilan Agro-Économique de l'Aménagement des Marais de Vilaine* (1983).

ONC-CREBS, *Anatidés et Zones Humides: Fascicule V: Valeurs Écologiques, Socio-culturelles et Économiques* (1981).

Scott, D. A., *A Preliminary Inventory of Wetlands of International Importance for Waterfowl in West Europe and Northwest Africa* (IWRB, 1980).
Secrétariat de la Faune et de la Flore, *Programmes d'Inventaires, Réseau Faune-flore et Publications* (1988).

# 5

# SPAIN

Carlos Montes and Pablo Bifani

## Spanish wetlands: an overview and historical perspective

The Iberian Peninsula has one of the richest and most diverse endowments of natural shallow-water environments in the EC. Although the natural surface area of wetlands in Spain is not as large as in other countries, some of the specific types found in Spain are unique to western Europe. This is particularly so for the steppe wetlands, which constitute one of the characteristic features of the Iberian landscape. Moreover, the geographical location of the Iberian peninsula allows it to serve as a bridge between Europe and north Africa. This makes Spanish wetlands key areas along the migration routes of several million waterfowl of the Western Paleartic. Many rare or endangered plant and animal species also make their habitat in Spanish wetlands.

In spite of the importance of Spanish wetlands, they are among the most threatened ecosystems in Spain. Nevertheless, a significant number of coastal and inland wetlands have been well conserved. The relatively low degree of economic development has led to reduced pressure on the natural environment in Spain, compared with other European countries. However, there are still several significant examples in Spain of serious wetland management problems, for example Daimiel, Doñana and Santoña.

Attempts to reclaim lowlands, either permanently or semi-permanently, have occurred throughout Spanish history. Since early times, different techniques have been used for wetland desiccation and alteration. Several periods can be distinguished.

The first period, lasting until the nineteenth century, was characterized by the fighting of paludism, a widespread water-borne disease in the Mediterranean and central regions of the Iberian Peninsula. Drainage projects initiated in the late eighteenth and early nineteenth century met with little success, due to the primitive nature of the techniques being used. During the eighteenth century, the wetlands of the Mediterranean coast underwent an important transformation, due to the proliferation of rice fields. On one hand, rice cultivation aggravated the problem of paludism. On the other hand, it created an opportunity for human and natural uses of wetlands to co-exist.

A second period lasted from about 1860 until the end of the civil war. Many wetlands were altered by drainage projects, especially those which were regarded as unhealthy, and which seemed to be of high potential for agriculture. Shallow-water environments were expressly defined as unproductive resources, which should be transformed in the national interest. During this period, unlike some other European countries, Spain lacked industrial development. Agriculture was therefore the major economic activity in the country. For the first time, wetland drainage objectives appeared in the Water Act of 1886, also remaining in the modified versions of 1879 and 1927. The drainage or filling of coastal wetlands was also expressly encouraged by the Harbours Law of 1927.

A third phase, lasting from just after the civil war to the present day, is characterized by the development and use of the natural environment based solely on economic criteria, largely disregarding the environmental processes which occur in these ecosystems.

Since 1936, agricultural policy has been oriented towards the "colonization" of wetlands by means of irrigation schemes and other mechanical techniques. The hydric resources of the Iberian Peninsula are unevenly distributed in both time and space. For this reason, an important programme of reservoir construction was initiated, essentially to supply water for agricultural irrigation projects. Reservoir construction increased rapidly from 1954 to 1970, with an increase from 200 to (the present) 889 reservoirs. In the 1950s, this policy was combined with projects to drain and reclaim several important wetlands for irrigated agriculture – La Mancha floodplains, Laguna de La Janda, Laguna de La Nava, Laguna de Antela, Marismas del Guadalquivir, and others. Many of these interventions were privately promoted, but were ultimately supported by the state. Despite the fact that paludism had already been eliminated, health and agricultural interests were both used as justifications for these projects. New technology and machinery made the drainages permanent.

The "colonization policy" was complemented, since 1952, by a reorganization of land tenure. Small-property ownership was consolidated into large holdings to permit the intensification of agricultural techniques. This resulted in increased application of machinery, fertilizers, and pesticides.

In recent years (especially since 1960), Spanish coastal wetland losses have been largely due to the evolution of the tourism industry. In 1984, 43 million people visited Spain (the second largest figure in Europe after Italy) gravitating mostly to beach areas. Tourism has developed into an important source of foreign currency for the country (US$8150 million in 1985). As a result, intense competition for land has developed in many coastal areas, especially along the Mediterranean shores such as the Costa Brava, Costa Dorada, Costa del Azahar, Costa Blanca, Costa del Sol and the Balearic Islands). These areas quickly became characterized by urban chaos, usually lacking important environmental services. This process continued during the 1970s and 1980s in most coastal regions, resulting in the disappearance of many hectares of coastal wetlands (Mar Menor, Aiguamolls de L'Empordà, Delta del Llobregat, Albufera de Alcudia, and others).

Industrialization was relatively slow until the 1960s. Most of the important industrial centres which exist today are located in coastal areas. Some of these affect wetlands directly. Examples include the Marismas del Tinto y del Odiel, which are among the most productive in the world, and which are now exposed to contamination from nearby factories. The transformation of coastal wetlands into rice fields also took place during this period. Rice areas increased from 35 000 ha in 1900, to 78 476 ha in 1986. This expansion was particularly important in the Guadalquivir marshes, in the Albufera de Valencia and in the Ebro Delta.

Environmental awareness in western countries grew during

the 1970s. However, only a few new conservation measures were implemented in Spain during this period. The Hunting Law and the Protected Natural Sites Law, which provided some degree of protection for a few shallow-water environments, are two examples.

The net result is that approximately sixty per cent of the Spanish wetland surface area is estimated to have been lost. This figure is unevenly distributed among the different types of wetland. In particular, large areas of fresh or mineralized water wetlands – for example floodplains, non-saline steppe shallow lakes, fluvio-marine marshes – have been totally or partially transformed. On the other hand, the saline shallow lakes, one of the most valuable environmental types which exist in Spain, remain in relatively good condition.

## Definition of wetlands

A generally-accepted definition of what constitutes Spanish "wetlands" is difficult to find. Actually, there are as many definitions of wetlands as there are scientists who have studied them. Since 1971, the most frequently used definition has been the one adopted by the Ramsar Convention: "Areas of marsh, fens, peatlands or waters whether natural or artificial, permanent or temporary with water that is static or flowing, fresh, brackish or salt, including areas of marine waters the depth of which at low tide does not exceed six meters."

For practical purposes, this definition is rather limited. Non-standardized terms – marsh, fens, peatlands, fresh, brackish – each have different meanings and can each be applied to a wide variety of wetland situations. The Ramsar definition is of limited application because it derives from an interest in wetlands primarily as waterfowl habitats. Clearly, the role of wetlands is broader than this. Actually, the ecological processes taking place in wetlands make them economically and environmentally important far beyond the spatial limits of the wetlands themselves. Thus, a more holistic definition, such as the US Wildlife Service's concept of wetlands as indicators of a set of ecological processes related to the presence of hydrophytes and hydric soils seems to be more appropriate (Cowardin et al. 1979).

For the Spanish national wetland inventory, the following operational definition has been adopted:

> Wetlands are non-flowing natural water-bodies of marine or continental origin (reported on the military map of Spain at a scale of 1:50 000 and in aerial photography at a scale of 1:18 000 and more than 0.5 ha in size). Lakes (deeper water habitats), although not wetlands themselves, are included as a separate section of the inventory for practical and managerial reasons.
>
> (Montes, 1990)

This definition seems to suit the basic goal of the inventory, which is to report the most important lentic water-bodies for conservation purposes.

Unlike the situation in most EC and OECD countries, a legal definition of wetlands is contained in the 1986 Water Act. Unfortunately, wetland scientists and managers did not participate in the elaboration of this definition. The result was the following very narrow concept of wetlands:

> Shallow-water environments, including artificial ones, will be considered as wetland. The following areas are included in this concept:
>
> (a) Permanent or temporary marshes, peatlands, or shallow waters formed by lotic or lentic, fresh, brackish or saline waters of natural or artificial origin.
>
> (b) Areas adjacent to the above-mentioned waters are also included, whenever necessary to avoid serious damages to nearby flora and fauna, if so decided by the legal and administrative authority.

This legal definition is very similar to that of the Ramsar Convention, but it is too broad and vague to assist in the classification, inventory, and delineation of wetlands. And yet, these activities are specifically contemplated by the new law. The Act also includes natural deep-water habitats (such as lakes), together with artificial reservoirs, as hydrological management units distinct from wetlands (Gonzalez Pérez et al., 1987). The Act does not include wetlands of marine origin, because its scope is limited to continental waters.

Mistch and Gosselink (1986) point out that the consistency with which a definition of wetlands is followed is just as important as the definition itself. Based on this idea, and using an ecological perspective, Bernaldez and Montes (1989) coined the following concept: wetlands are *any* functional unit of the landscape that is neither a lake nor a river; that represents a spatial and temporary positive hydric anomaly in relation to a drier surrounding land; and that is important enough to affect adjacent life processes.

This definition uses the presence of hydrophytes and hydric soils as basic elements in the definition of wetlands, but adds the existence of a peculiar flora/fauna and specific human uses which are different from those prevailing in adjacent spaces. The concept includes a gradient from "hidden seepages", or areas in which only the root-zone of the vegetation is moistened by the upper limit of the saturated layer (wet meadows, sedge meadows, phreatophytic woodlands, and so on). It also includes limnological types of water bodies that are periodically or permanently flooded with shallow water (ponds, bogs, sloughs, marshes, peatlands, lagoons, pools, floodplains, deltas, salinas, playa lakes, and so on). However, this concept *excludes* deep-water habitats, such as lakes, which are characterized by the regular occurrence of thermal stratification in layers of different densities.

## The national wetland inventory

Unlike some other OECD countries (for example the United States), where wetland inventories were first conducted to develop local agricultural potential through drainage and land-reclamation activities, the first Spanish inventory made by the Ministry of Agriculture towards the end of 1940s had a more conservationist character (Pardo, 1948).

The relatively large extent of American wetlands made them attractive for alternative uses, so the conversion of natural wetlands into agricultural land was often an explicitly-stated objective. In the Spanish case, the relatively small extent of wetlands did *not* make them particularly attractive for alternative uses. The potential benefits of their conversion were considered at that time to be insufficient to compensate for the costs involved. Thus, the management of wetlands in such a way as to benefit from their economic and cultural values was often a more suitable alternative. Conversion often did occur in Spain, but was not typically an *a priori* management goal.

The Ministry of Agriculture did not make any other attempt to inventory wetlands until the middle of 1970s. This was not a full inventory but a sort of "state of the situation" (Velez, 1979). Several regional inventories with different objectives, and using different wetland concepts, have also been undertaken in recent years.

The various inventories made during the last decade have concentrated on the waterfowl habitat function of wetlands. These inventories provided a short list of natural wetlands, and a large one of artificial reservoirs. By emphasizing the extent of artificial reservoirs, which tend to harm wetlands, the inventories produced an incorrect image of the real importance of natural Spanish wetlands.

A comprehensive inventory of Spanish wetlands was initiated in 1988 under the guidance of an interdisciplinary team of scientists. The objective of this project is to prepare a complete list of wetlands to guide the design of policy for their conservation and rational use. However, the inventory does not include hidden seepages, or the wetlands of the Spanish islands (Baleares and Canarias), which fall under separate administrative jurisdictions.

Since the national inventory has not yet been completed, it is not possible to provide detailed figures concerning the quantity of natural wetlands. Preliminary estimates suggest that there are about twenty thousand such units. Only about two thousand of those units are larger than 0.5 ha. About thirty per cent of these units belong to a single wetland type – that of the high mountain lakes of the Pyrenees. (Deep-water habitats are included in the inventory for administrative convenience, rather than to suggest that these are really "wetlands" in the common usage of the term. Statistics on Spanish wetlands are, therefore, biased by the inclusion of these habitats in the data.)

The original wet surface of the country is estimated at between 400 000 and 500 000 ha, or about one per cent of the national territory. Between 50 and 60 per cent of the total Spanish wetland surface area relates to one of the few large wetland systems – Marismas del Guadalquivir; Aiguamolls de l'Emporda; Bahía de Cádiz; Delta del Ebro; Mar Menor; Albufera de Valencia.

## Wetland types

Not much research has been done to classify Spanish wetlands, even though the Iberian Peninsula is an excellent location for this type of study, due to the large number and diversity of its shallow non-fluent waters. Alonso and Comelles (1981, 1984) and Alonso (1985, 1987) were the first to develop the basis of a regional limnology of Spanish wetlands using a classification that takes salinity, turbidity, flooding regimes and relation with the presence or absence of specific biological communities into account.

### *Inland wetlands*

Several types of inland wetlands are found in Spain. For example, *permanent or semi-permanent wetlands in high mountains* include ponds, sloughs, and wet meadows, and provide special environmental conditions for aquatic life. Most of these basins are of glacial origin. They typically freeze over for several months each year. In semi-permanent and temporary wetlands, biological communities are adapted for seasonal freezing tolerances, but not for drought. They have clean freshwaters and are normally less than two metres deep. This wetland type is usually found above 1500 m in the main mountain ranges, and in some other mountain areas on northern-oriented slopes.

*Permanent or temporary wetlands at low and medium altitudes* typically have the same ecological characteristics as those at higher altitudes, except that the winter period is not usually cold or long enough to force aquatic organisms to develop special tolerances. Wetlands of this type occur below 1500 m in areas with more than 600–700 mm of annual rainfall. Ercina Lake (9 ha) in Covadonga National Park is a good example.

*Non-saline steppe wetlands* include temporary ponds – vernal or autumnal pools – and shallow lakes, with variable basin size, whose waters are more or less mineralized. They can be either clean or muddy, and are usually less than one metre deep. Turbidity and the duration of drought periods are the most relevant ecological factors determining the composition and structure of the aquatic communities. The basins tend to have very different origins – karstic, phreatic, aeolic, volcanic, tectonic, fluvial.

This is the most abundant type among inland Spanish wetlands (53 per cent), and is found most often in endorheic (semi-arid) areas, which receive less than 600–700 mm of rainfall. These are especially numerous in the Douro, Ebro, Guadiana and Guadalquivir river basins. The most important examples of this type are the Medina (Cádiz), Nava Grande (Ciudad Real), Hito (Cuenca) and Pitillas (Navarra) shallow lakes.

*Shallow inland saline lakes* (lowest salinity greater than 10 per cent) are a common feature in the landscapes of the semi-arid regions of three of the four large sedimentary Tertiary basins – Ebro, Gualdalquivir and Tajo Trough – situated on marine or continental evaporites. These systems are unique in the EC.

There are approximately sixty-six Spanish saline lakes distributed in 14 endorheic nuclei, with salinity ranges between 10 and 430 per cent, and a surface of approximately 4800 ha (Montes and Martino, 1987). Nearly all of these wetlands are temporary, except the Salada de Chiprana (Zaragoza), which is about five metres deep. Their flora and fauna are characterized by a paucity of species, but many are of great environmental value. In highly saline lakes (gamma-hypersaline water), there is no animal life, and only halobacteria communities can survive. Temporality, salinity gradient, and ionic composition are the most important ecological variables for aquatic life in this type of wetland. The most important examples are Gallocanta, Fuente de Piedra, Manjavacas, Playa, Peña Hueca and Petrola.

*Dune field wetlands* are a very peculiar wetland type that occurs basically in the dune systems of Doñana National Park, and in some adjacent areas. They are temporary and permanent ponds (non-marine lagoons). They are flooded by seepages in the downs, where the water table rises above the surface. In semi-arid areas, some inland sand dunes exist with semi-permanent ponds (Douro river basin). Their waters are fresh, with very low mineralization. The permanence of the water, and the degree of eutrophy or dystrophy, are the most important ecological factors affecting aquatic life.

The most significant examples of this type are found in the dune complexes of Doñana National Park (Santa Ollalla, Dulce and Taraje lagoons); in the El Abalario complex; in the Cantalejo lagoons in the Douro river basin; and in the Corrubedo ponds of Galicia.

*Floodplains and peri-riverine complexes* encompass semi-arid wetlands of very different characteristics associated with fluvial and groundwater processes. This type includes flood-plains next to river channels (which are flooded during high-water periods); old meanders; and inland deltas related to aquifer discharge zones.

The most important wetlands of this type are some floodplains along the Guadiana river, and in the Tablas de Daimiel National Park, both located in La Mancha region. In this area, floodplains account for more than 25 000 ha.

*Peat deposits* are not extensive in Spain. Spanish mires are mainly distributed in three sectors situated in northern, central and eastern (Levante) regions. Most of these are high mires of small geographic area, less than 100 ha, and are not very deep (less than 4 m). The larger ones are lowland mires. The most important areas of this type are the peatlands of Daimiel, Torreblanca and Padul. The total surface area of Spanish peatlands is estimated at 6700 ha.

*Inland salinas* are associated with springs situated in Keuper geological grounds, where small flooded areas have been used since ancient times for halite exploitation. There are about fifty of these salinas in Spain, most of them of small (less than 5 ha), and often abandoned. Important ones are those of Gerri de la Sal (Lérida); Belinchon (Cuenca); and Pinilla (Albacete). The water found in the salt pans of the salinas supports the only type of permanent hypersaline water-bodies in Spain, which is the habitat of very valuable flora and fauna.

*Wadi complexes* are ephemeral streams of arid regions that may occasionally be exorheic in the less arid sectors, or near the coast. Wadis are of interest, not as watercourses, but as wetland habitats that result from the frequent groundwater seepages, pools or shallow waterbodies found in their normally dry channels. The most important wadi complexes are located in the provinces of Murcia and Almería.

## *Coastal wetlands*

Coastal wetlands represent almost 80 per cent of the total Spanish wetland area.

*Fluvio-marine marshes* are tidal saltmarshes found along the Atlantic coast. Biological communities in this class of wetlands are well-adapted to the stresses of changes in salinity, periodic inundation, and extreme temperatures. The most important are Marismas del Odiel y Tinto; Bahía de Cádiz; Ortigueira and Santoña. Some of these areas have been largely transformed into coastal salinas for halite exploitation, for example Bahía de Cádiz.

A special wetland of this type is former tidal saltmarshes which have evolved geomorphologically, so that direct connections with the ocean have been cut. The only water sources are rainfall, river inputs and direct discharges from aquifers. The duration of flooding, combined with the spatial and seasonal distribution of salinity, are the most important ecological factors affecting aquatic life. These are temporary systems, in which flooding cycles have seasonal, rather than daily, dimensions. They can be defined as temporary saltmarshes, even though they contain fresh water during the beginning of the hydrological cycle. This type of wetland is found in the Guadalquivir river marshes, the largest of Spanish wetlands.

*Fluvial marshes* include freshwater marshes – aiguamolls, ullals, marjales – located along the Mediterranean coast. They include the mouths of small rivers and aquifer discharges. They are not subject to significant tidal influences, because tides are not very high along this coast. The most representative examples of this class are the Prat de Cabanes-Torreblanca; the Marjal de Oliva-Pego; and the Aiguamolls de l'Emporda.

Most Spanish *coastal lagoons* are located along the Mediterranean shore, where the tidal range is small. The Mar Menor, La Albufera de Valencía and the Ebro Delta are the most important examples of this type of wetland. The degree of connection with marine waters, and the quantity/quality of freshwater inputs, determine the distribution of their biotic and abiotic characteristics in both time and space. Several Spanish Mediterranean coastal lagoons have been transformed long ago for halite exploitation, for example the lagoons of Torrevieja, Santa Pola and Cabode Gata.

## Wetland management institutions

### *The legal framework*

Until 1985, the use of continental waters in Spain was regulated by the Water Act of 1879. This Act included the Cambo Law (1918), which specifically grouped lagoons and shallow waters under the general heading of "unhealthy areas". Such a negative concept of wetlands also lay behind the establishment of different measures to promote drainage and land reclamation. Tax incentives and other forms of economic incentive were often used to achieve this objective. The enactment of several different types of laws (since abolished) such as the Port Act of 1928; the Shores Act of 1969; and the Coastal Protection Act of 1980; and the 1973 Act of Land Reform and Agriculture Development, resulted in a rather chaotic legal situation surrounding wetlands. Against the background of this legal framework, important Spanish wetlands were drained or reclaimed, generally after 1960.

Several other Acts are still in effect which also exert an indirect influence over wetlands. The most noteworthy of these are the Patrimonio National Act of 1933; the Hunting Act of 1970; the River Fishing Act of 1942; and the special Plans for the Protection of the Physical Environment, included in the Soil Act of 1956 and its revision of 1975. Between 1975 and 1989, it was possible to protect areas of special environmental value, like wetlands, by resorting to the Natural Spaces Protection Act, which regulated access to the use of natural environments and includes National Parks; Integral Reserves of Scientific Interest; Natural Parks; and Natural Landscapes of National Interest. However, administrative difficulties limited the effectiveness of this law, so very few wetlands were actually protected by them.

The new Water Act (1985) is based on three principles:

(i) the public character of continental waters (both surficial and groundwater);
(ii) the need for planning to follow the hydrologic cycle; and
(iii) the public administration of water resources according to a hydrographic basin structure.

In addition, conservation objectives are now explicitly included to protect wetlands – National Wetland Inventory, Wetland Rehabilitation, Environmental Impact Assessment, Water Quality Control, and others. However, the narrow and vague definition of the concept of "wetland", as previously discussed, combined with continuing incentives to drain wetlands under specific circumstances, effectively reduces these "rules" to little more than declarations of principle (Martínez–Parra, 1988a).

In 1989, Parliament also approved The Conservation of Natural Spaces Act and the Flora and Fauna Wildlife Act, which replaced the Natural Protected Space Act of 1975. The new law, for which exact rules have yet to be approved, establishes that watershed planning must include consideration for the conservation and recovery of wetlands. It also perceives the preparation, and continuous updating, of a wetland inventory.

The Shore Act of 1988 protects unaltered coastal areas, including wetlands.

In addition to national legislation, it is also necessary to consider laws enacted by each of the Autonomous Communities. At present, only two of the seventeen Autonomous Communities have enacted special laws for the protection of natural spaces: Cataluña in 1984, and Andalucía in 1989.

Since the 1960s, wetland protection objectives in Spain have been pursued largely for the sake of waterfowl (Fernández-Cruz, 1987). In other words, the protection criteria that were adopted disregarded the other values of wetland ecosystems. This bias is also an indication of the lobbying power of certain organizations, such as the Spanish Society of Ornithology (SEO). It also reflects the growing desire for Spanish wetland management programmes to be better integrated into global programmes for bird protection, such as those promoted by the International Council for Bird Preservation (ICBP), and the International Waterfowl and Wetland Research Bureau (IWWRB).

Even when broader ecologic objectives *are* recognized, biases can enter into policy priorities. For example, wetlands located in mountainous or forested landscapes, and those with large areas or game resources have both been favoured in conservation programmes, while wetlands located in dry, endorheic portions of the flatlands have remained largely ignored (Montes and Martín de Agar, 1989).

Another common bias is the lack of attention paid to the

geological, geomorphological, geochemical and hydrological aspects of wetland ecosystems.

The conservation of wetlands, (indeed, of all natural spaces) is typically subordinated to the prevailing fashions or perceptions of each historic period. Consequently, the first wetlands protected in Spain – Covadonga and Aigues Tortes National Parks – were those where social preferences for alpine and subalpine landscapes could be met. After the civil war, hunting objectives dominated the protection of open spaces, through the Game Refuges, which include wetlands. Environmental concerns of the 1970s and 1980s are, in their turn, reflected in rules creating Natural Parks and Reserves of Scientific Interest, and in the use of hunting regulation standards to promote the rapid implementation of conservation measures.

The net result of this *ad hoc* approach has been the absence of many valuable wetlands from Spanish conservation programmes. This is particularly true for some extreme environments (hypersaline or hyperalkaline water-bodies, peatlands); for areas not especially valuable for waterfowl production (karstic or high mountain lakes); or for areas that did not fit with commonly accepted aesthetic patterns (steppe wetlands). Fortunately, this attitude is now changing, and new research programmes are emerging, based on a holistic approach, rather than only on landscape or biological criteria.

## *The administrative framework*

Since the Spanish Constitution was approved in 1978, environmental matters have been administered by both the Central State Administration, and the Regional Administrations of the Autonomous States. There are at least 15 different General Directions within five Ministries – Public Works and Urbanism; Industry and Energy; Public Health; Agriculture, Fishing and Food; Transport, Tourism and Communications – dealing with the environment. Nature conservation and protection of natural resources in Spain is the responsibility of the 17 Autonomous States in co-operation with a central body, the Institute for the Conservation of Nature (ICONA) established in 1971. This agency is located within the Ministry of Agriculture, Fishing and Food and mostly provides policy co-ordination and advice. It also manages the National Parks.

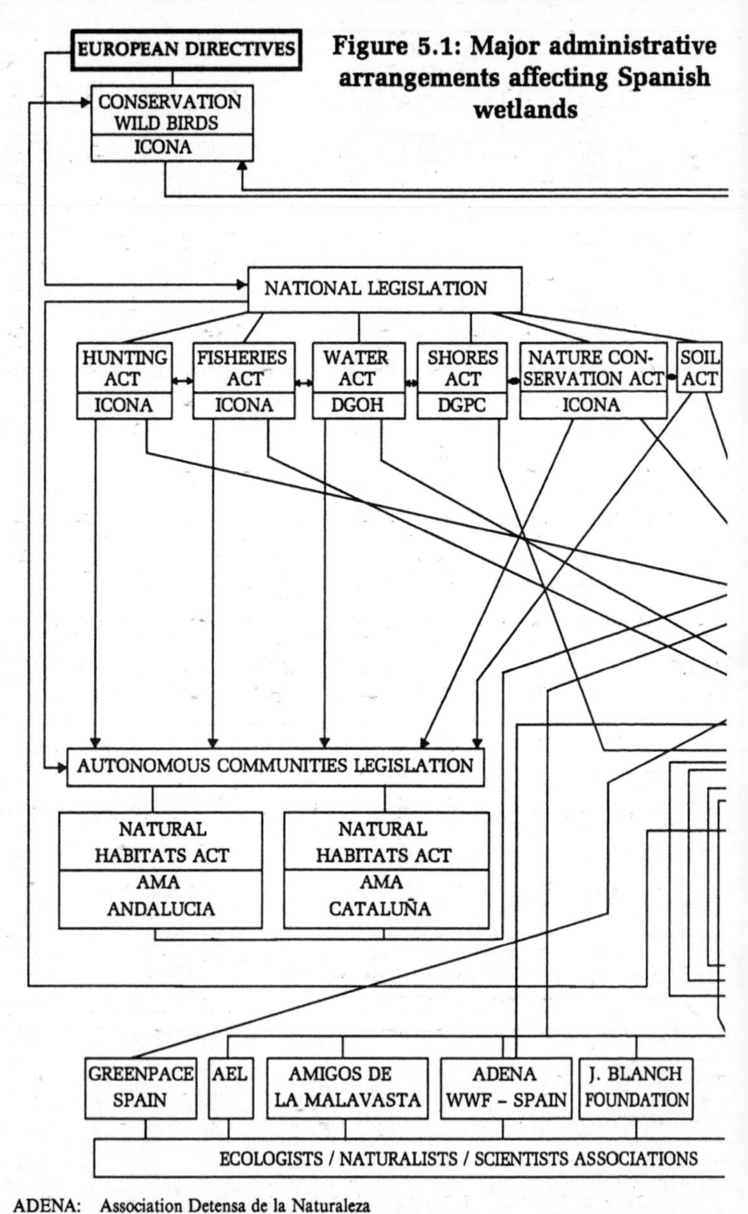


**Figure 5.1: Major administrative arrangements affecting Spanish wetlands**

ADENA: Association Detensa de la Naturaleza
ICONA: Instituto Nacional para la Conservación de la Naturaleza: Ministerio de Agricultura,
DGOH: Dirección General de Obras Hidraulicas: Ministerio de Obras Públicas y Urbanismo
DGMA: Dirección General de Medio Ambiente: Ministerio de Obras Públicas y Urbanismo
DGPC: Dirección General de Puertos y Costas: Ministerio de Obras Públicas y Urbanismo
AMA: Agencia del Medio Ambiente
PNUMA: United Nations Environment Programme

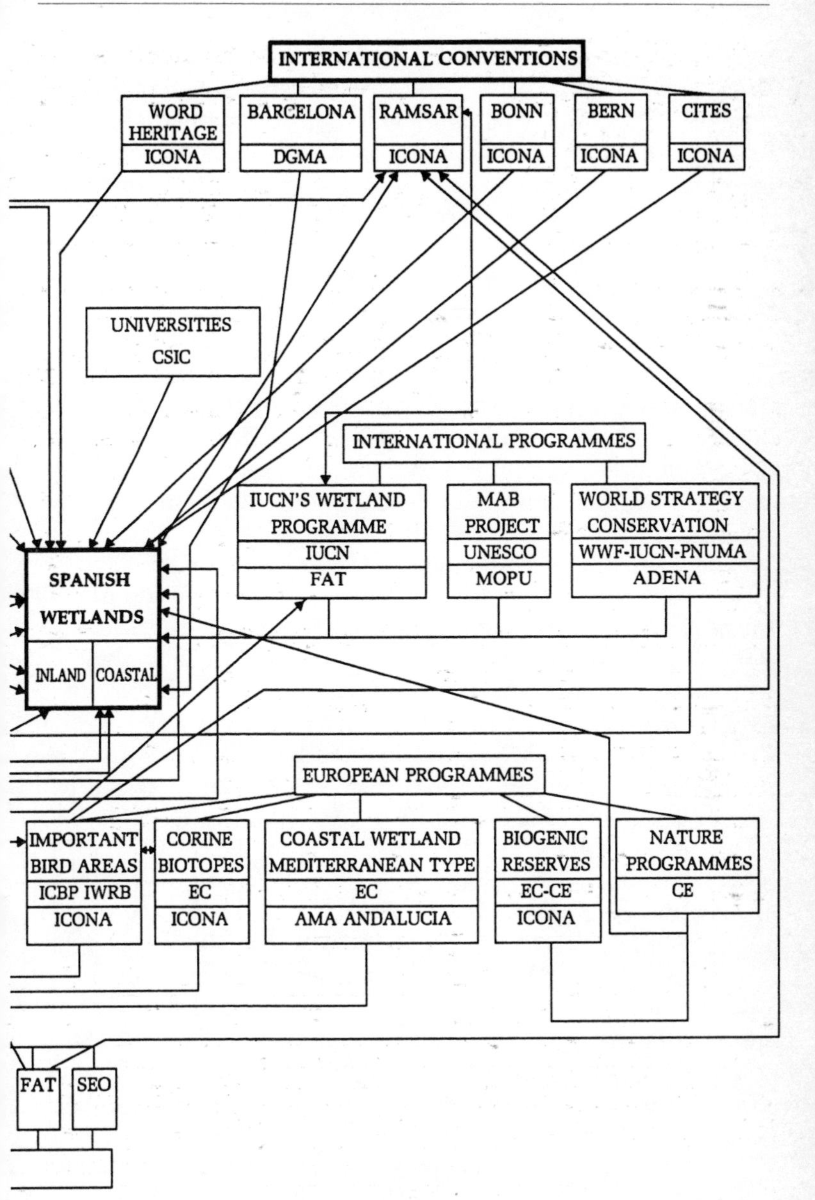


Pesca y Alimentación

MAB: Man and the Biosphere
CSIC: Consejo Sueperior Investigaciones Clientificas
SEO: Asociación Española de Ortinologia
AEL: Asociación Española de Limnologia
FAT Federación Amigos de la Tierra
IUCN: International Union for the Conservation of Nature

Another important agency is the General Secretariat for the Environment (DGMA) set up in 1978 within the Ministry of Public Works and Urbanism. This Secretariat is in charge of basic legislation projects, environmental impact assessment studies, environmental education, and international relations. Both ICONA and DGMA are housed in ministries where other programme activities could potentially harm the environment.

Only a few Autonomous States – Andalucía, Asturias, Murcia, Madrid – have institutionalized co-ordination within their environmental protection and conservation mandates by establishing Environment Agencies. Andalucía is clearly the Autonomous State most concerned with wetland protection, having a high number of legally-protected areas with restrictions for economic uses (Natural Reserves). Paradoxically, Andalucía is one of the least developed Autonomous States in economic terms (Diaz del Olmo and Molina, 1985).

The result of this fragmentation is an administrative structure which is totally unable to deal with the increasing complexity of modern environmental problems. Figure 5.1 illustrates the complex system of jurisdictions that affect Spanish wetlands.

Another negative factor was the abolition of the Inter-Ministries Commission for the Environment (CIMA), which had been in charge of co-ordinating all administrative bodies concerned with environmental matters. Its abolition resulted in political interests dominating what should be essentially ecological debates.

In summary, Spain has ratified most of the international conventions, programmes and directives governing the protection of natural resources in Europe. Spain also already has in place a proper legal framework for the protection of its own wetlands. Nevertheless, the multiplicity of management responsibilities, and a general lack of legislative co-ordination both result in significant administrative confusion. A gap in the formulation and implementation of national policy on wetland conservation and development policy is the inevitable result.

## *International measures*

The Convention on Wetlands of International Importance Especially as Waterfowl Habitat, known more simply as the Ramsar Convention, is the only international treaty dedicated to the conservation of a particular ecosystem type. Having no legal authority over the governments of the 51 member countries, the Treaty involves only moral suasion. Nevertheless, it has become an important conservation tool. For example, it played an important role in the government's decision to take measures leading to the hydric restoration of the Tablas de Daimiel National Park (Troya, 1989).

Currently, 20 Spanish wetlands are included under Ramsar, covering a total area of 101 000 ha. These particular wetlands were designated under the Ramsar rubric largely because of their values as waterfowl habitats. Efforts are now being made to include other natural sites because of high values for different ornithological populations, for example Lagunas de Corrubedo, Ría de Gernika.

EC resolutions concerning conservation of wetlands as habitats for many wild bird species are another important aspect of the international dimension of Spanish wetlands. The Directive and Resolution of the Council of the European Community on the Conservation of Wild Birds was ratified by Spain in 1986. Seventeen wetland complexes in Spain have since been declared as special protection areas under this directive.

Several other international agreements regarding natural areas, habitats or species protection have also been ratified by Spain:

- The Convention Concerning the Protection of the World Cultural and Natural Heritage (The World Heritage Convention) came into force in 1975, and has since been ratified by Spain;
- The Convention for the Protection of the Mediterranean Sea against Pollution (The Barcelona Convention), and the Protocol Concerning Mediterranean Specially-Protected Areas were both signed by Spain. (The Protocol has not yet been ratified by the Spanish Parliament);
- The Convention on International Trade of Endangered Flora and Fauna Wildlife Species (the CITES or Washington Convention) was ratified by Spain in 1985;
- The Convention on the Conservation of Migratory Species of Wild Animals (Bonn Convention) was ratified by Spain in 1985; and
- The Convention on the Conservation of European Wildlife

and Natural Habitat (Bern Convention) was ratified by Spain in 1986.

Some of the most important wetland management and conservation programmes developed by international organizations, and in which Spain participates, are:

- UNESCO's Man and the Biosphere (MAB) Programme (Project no. 8) on the conservation of natural areas and the genetic material they contain. MAB Project no. 5 also deals with the ecological effects of human activities on lakes, marshes, rivers, estuaries and coastal zones;
- The International Union for the Conservation of Nature (IUCN) launched a programme in 1985 to integrate wetland conservation and socio-economic development in all countries of the Union;
- the Important Bird Areas in Europe Programme, developed by the International Council for Bird Preservation (ICBP), and the International Waterfowl and Wetlands Research Bureau (IWRB), provide key information on sites of major importance for the conservation of Europe's avifauna, including many Spanish wetlands; and
- the World Conservation Strategy was approved by the Spanish government in 1980.

Some EC programmes also directly affect the conservation of Spanish wetlands:

- The European Network of Biogenic Reserves was launched in 1976, with the aim of preserving representative examples of Europe's fauna, flora and natural areas;
- The Biotopes Project of the CORINE Programme develops a databank concerning the location and characteristics of EC habitats which are important for nature conservation, including wetlands; and
- The Integrated Management of Coastal Wetlands of Mediterranean Type programme also implicates Spanish coastal wetlands.

And finally, there are several scientific, conservation, or environmental organizations within Spain itself, which are involved in wetlands conservation and management. These groups have played an important role in generating public action in favour of nature protection, even though their efforts are not normally organized into formal "programmes". For example, some groups in Spanish universities, as well as the National Council for Scientific Research (CSIC) are devoted to conserving Spain's wetland heritage.

## Major functions and values of Spanish wetlands

### *Environmental values*

It is generally accepted that the most important role played by wetlands is closely related to their function as part of natural *hydrological processes*, for example flood mitigation, aquifer discharge, erosion control. These systems serve as indicators of the degree of water conservation (quality and quantity) needed for a given region. In Spain, wetlands do not play as important a role in flood attenuation as they do in other countries, due to the high degree of regulation offered by the many reservoirs which exist. On the other hand, many Spanish wetlands are important sources of groundwater. They are also extremely vulnerable to over-exploitation.

Vegetation also plays a considerable role in reducing and controlling local soil erosion. Spain suffers one of the highest erosion risks in Europe. Twenty-five per cent of Spanish territory is regularly affected by erosion, especially in semi-arid regions (DGMA, 1986).

Because of its geographic location, bridging Europe and Africa, Spain is the crossing point of several biogeographical regions. The country also possesses great environmental diversity – landform, geological history, climate, lithology, hydrology. As a result, Spain is rich in rare species of fauna and flora. Spanish wetlands are very important as *habitat* for a variety of animals and plants, some of which have a very high environmental value. Especially interesting in this regard are the steppe wetlands which retain old fauna and flora similar to those found in north Africa and central Asia.

Some research has been done on the environmental dangers

associated with the extinction of some of the species found in Spanish wetlands. Different groups of hydrophytes, invertebrates, waterfowl, fish, and other vertebrates depend completely on wetlands for their food, protection, breeding, resting and/or other life-giving requirements (Morillo, 1986).

Spanish wetlands are probably best known internationally for their abundance and variety of waterfowl. They are very important sites for wintering and resting in the migratory movements and breeding for many European bird populations. An estimated 42 per cent of waterfowl using Spanish wetlands (95 species) belong to some of the categories of endangered species (Martin-Novella et al., 1988; Fernández-Cruz et al., 1988).

Wetlands take organic and inorganic nutrients, including toxic materials, out of the water they contain, under certain circumstances. Thanks to this process, some Spanish wetlands still retain a high degree of environmental quality, in spite of often suffering significant loadings of domestic, industrial and agricultural wastes. Some examples of this process are the shallow steppe lakes of Manjavacas and Pedro Muñoz; the fluvio-marine marshes of Odiel and Tinto; and the coastal lagoon of Mar Menor.

## *Economic values*

*Recreation and education activities*, for example hiking, nature observation, phototography, swimming and boating, are significant in many Spanish wetlands. Some have been used for the implementation of nature experience and environmental education programmes. As one example, Doñana National Park was visited by more than 40 000 people in 1987. This was an important source of tourism income in the region (although, admittedly, not as important as tourism in areas surrounding the Park).

Spanish wetlands traditionally support a valuable *recreational hunting* industry related to waterfowl. The hunting season coincides with the annual migration of waterfowl through Spain. There is no comprehensive data about the value of waterfowl hunting in Spain, but together with other hunting activities, it is estimated to generate about 40 000 jobs and US$1500 million per year (Metra Seis, 1985). An estimated 1 300 000 hunters (321 000 with licences) operate in Spain. However, more and more wetland sites now have legal regulations that forbid this type of use, reflecting a growing management conflict.

Traditionally, *fishing* has been important only in coastal wetlands. Fishing used to be the main economic activity for many coastal communities such as Ebro Delta, Albufera de Valencía, Cádiz Bay, and so on. Increasingly, urban, industrial and agricultural pollution have combined to threaten, or even to eliminate, this traditional resource in some locations.

The Louisiana red crayfish (*Procambarus clarkii*) was introduced, in 1974, into the Guadalquivir marshes. Since its introduction, this species has become an important fishery resource. In Seville province alone, 3 000 000 kg, valued at US$6.5 million, were collected in 1982. (However, environmental problems associated with this species have also increased.)

*Aquaculture* – fish, crustaceans, and brineshrimp – is an important use of coastal salinas, especially in the Cádiz Bay area, where salt pans extend over 8000 ha. Some other wetland species of plants or animals were economically important in earlier times, for example frog, eel, otter, chelonians, reed, soft rush, and bulrush. The latter species were used for food and in the basket and chair industries, or as building materials (Pardo, 1942).

Many inland and coastal wetlands have an ionic composition that makes them suitable for *mineral extraction*. Some saline shallow lakes and inland salinas have been used, and some still are, for salt extraction. Halite extraction was originally an important industry in Cádiz Bay, and along the Mediterranean shore. Today, it is not a very profitable activity, due to reduced markets. Most of the salt pans have been transformed for fish culture, where high productivity leads to better economic prospects. The highly-mechanized salt production system of Torrevieja is one of the most important in Europe, yielding 1 000 000 Tm per year.

Some inland (Celadilla) and coastal (Mar Menor) areas are still used as *curative baths* for dermal and rheumatic illnesses.

An abundance of inland saline wetlands allows Spain to be unique in Europe in exploiting these wetlands for *biotechnology* (production of glycerol, B-carotenes, antibiotics), and bioengineering (Hammer, 1986).

### *Cultural values*

Because of the semi-arid climate that prevails in Spain, wetlands are attractive units of the *landscape* that contribute in an important way to the diversification of the scenery.

Spanish wetlands have also been an inspiration for important authors of Spanish literature, and have served as the origins of many legends and traditions which are part of the nation's *cultural heritage* (Montes and Martín de Agar, 1989).

### *Scientific values*

The abundance and diversity of natural and artificial wetlands in Spain constitute ideal conditions for performing many forms of scientific *research*, for example geological, geomorphological, sedimentological, ecological, physiological, paleolimnological, evolutive and biogeographical parameters.

## Market failure

A major problem encountered in any economic analysis of wetlands is that adequate ecological information is usually lacking, and even when it is available, it is not always feasible to translate this data into economic and monetary values. Thus, it is not only a problem of monetary valuation, but also that the full environmental role of wetlands is still poorly understood. Because the economic importance of wetlands has been recognized only very recently, the linkages between the environmental and ecological functions of wetland areas are only now beginning to be seriously examined.

Another difficulty arises from the existence of alternative possible uses of the wetland. For example, a given wetland can be exploited for fish production, for waste treatment, for residential development, for water use, and for recreation. When a wetland is used simultaneously for more than one purpose, it is even more difficult to estimate values for each of these uses.

The wide diversity in wetland ecological, physical, chemical and biological parameters forces policy-makers to examine each decision individually. In other words, "recipes" are not possible, and policies based on a single definition of wetlands are likely to be misleading.

A fundamental feature of wetlands is that they are in the process of transition from an aquatic to a terrestrial resource. This transitionality suggests that policy should emphasize the "unbounded" character and the functionality of wetland ecosystems. In turn, this suggests that the most suitable approach for analysing wetlands is a systemic one. However, the traditional approach has been to ignore this "systems dimension", focusing on only one, or a few, uses.

A system is composed of a number of static variables linked by operators, and then subjected to exogenous inputs and outputs. Understanding the transformation operators is especially important for understanding how the system actually works. Unbounded systems, like wetlands, cannot be considered apart from the dynamics of surrounding areas, with which they share components and processes. The complexity of this interrelationship is further magnified when the socio-economic system is overlain on the environmental system. In other words, the unbounded nature of wetlands has at least two major dimensions: one related to the interface with other natural systems and the second related to the interface with the socio-economic system. Economic interventions that create problems for wetlands can be viewed through several "optics".

First, the *form* of the intervention can be of many types – momentary duration; unit step; constant change; and so on. The intervention can also combine these forms, in which case the magnitude of its effects will be more difficult to predict, and the root cause of the perturbation more difficult to identify.

There are at least four *mechanisms* through which an intervention can take place. These are:

(i) extracting more output;
(ii) modifying the inputs;
(iii) manipulating the functional characteristics of the ecosystem (that is, acting on the transfer function); and
(iv) combining all three approaches.

Historically, most economic interventions in Spain have been focused on the mechanical relationship between inputs and outputs, and on the fact that certain types of inputs have the capacity to stimulate the system in a way that results in increased output. The natural system itself has been used as a "black-box", into which inputs are fed and output is harvested, largely ignoring how the former are transformed. In some cases, productivity has improved, but only by becoming entirely dependent on the intensive use of energetic inputs, such as water, energy, fertilizers, and chemical pesticides. In such a situation, the economic system will inevitably become increasingly artificialized over time. An important result of this type of intervention is that little is known about the transformation function, and therefore, about how policies to increase or decrease the input or output flows may actually work in practice.

Another factor to consider is the *time* it takes for changes induced by interventions to be felt. Variations in these rates depend upon the intervention itself; on the characteristics of the receptors; on the persistence of the introduced changes; and on the resilience of the system. A fundamental problem faced by environmental managers is how to balance temporal effects with spatial ones. This is particularly important in the case of wetlands because the unbounded nature of wetlands makes them especially prone to indirect effects of actions implemented in other systems for different purposes, and in different time periods.

All of the above are good reasons for not looking at economic intervention in wetlands only in terms of the direct actions affecting them. Some of the most serious disruptions of wetlands are caused by indirect effects. This problem complicates the design of policies for wetlands because it is difficult to identify the appropriate points of leverage, the key actors and the magnitude and time of occurrence of the expected effects.

Another methodological issue to be addressed refers to the fact that wetlands conversion entails costs and benefits that are not reflected by market prices, and that frequently these costs and benefits are experienced by third parties. In effect, the private costs and benefits of wetland use and transformations tend to diverge from the social costs and benefits, a divergence that is usually at the origin of social and economic conflicts. This is the well-known "externality problem". Externalities can be of two basic types.

First, they can result from pollution/degradation imposed by one economic actor on another. In the past, wetlands were considered to be unhealthy and barren lands, so *all* conversion was considered to be beneficial. However, today the environmental and economic values of wetlands ecosystems are increasingly being recognized, so the cost-benefit position is less clear. Unfortunately, the lack of monetary expression for many of the values of wetlands makes such assessments very difficult.

Second, externalities can result from the fact that wetlands are "public goods" for which private property rights are difficult to define and enforce. Consequently, an effective market for the exchange of their services does not exist. Although it is easy to establish property rights for plots of land, owning titles to underground water is an entirely different matter. Not only is it not possible to quantify the water which lies beneath each plot of land, it is also impossible to control it. In this situation, each owner of a plot of land can usually extract as much water as desired without any regard to the effects of that extraction on the owners of neighbouring parcels. It is well-known that this "riparian doctrine" encourages excessive rates of water extraction, leading, in some cases, to the eventual ruin of the basin. An example is Tablas de Daimiel.

In short, wetland market failure can be due to both *pollution* externalities and *property rights* externalities. There are strong reasons to believe that the property rights issue is more important than pollution externalities in many Spanish wetland cases.

## Intervention failure

Intervention failure can be classified as:

(i) intersectoral policy inconsistencies (which include favouring competing-sector output and input prices); and
(ii) incompatible land uses and counterproductive wetlands policies (which are mainly institutional-type failures).

It is usually difficult to isolate a single market or intervention failure that leads to a particular wetland loss. Losses are typically caused by a combination of both types of failures. In some cases, market failures predominate, while in others it is the intervention failure that is the main cause of the disruption. Moreover, one type of failure often leads to the other, magnifying its effects. For example, drainage subsidies for agricultural expansion (intervention failure) can be followed by resource over-exploitation (property rights externality, market failure) and pollution (pollution externality market failure).

Market failure can also often lead directly to intervention failure because the traditional policy response to market failure is to compensate the actors, not to address the root cause of the problem. Frequently, this compensation creates an entirely new set of problems of its own (intervention failure).

Even though the precise source of wetland losses cannot be specified in many cases, some obvious reasons for intervention failure stand out above the others.

## *Drainage*

As in other countries, the major cause of wetlands loss in Spain has been their conversion to agricultural use. This type of intervention failure generally results from deficient land use policy. Major examples include:

1 The *Ebro Delta* is the most important external deltaic complex in the Iberian peninsula. There were originally about thirty-two thousand hectares of wetlands in the delta. Agricultural transformation was first undertaken in the region during the eighteenth century. As a result, 77 per cent of the original surface is today under cultivation (24 000 ha; 15 000 ha for rice and 9500 for orchards). The natural hydrologic cycle has been altered so that most of the water flows in the delta now depend on human-controlled systems. The geological build-up of land in the delta has been interrupted, and there is even a land loss occurring in some places, due to the large-scale damming of the Ebro River. This damming has resulted in a 15 per cent decrease in waterflows, and sediments are trapped by the dams. The delta wetlands are a complex of fluvial marshes and coastal lagoons of international importance as habitat for many valuable species of fauna and flora. Human communities used to live

in balance with an integrated resource exploitation system – cultivation, fishing and hunting – but current projects to develop tourism facilities – urban areas, leisure harbours – are threatening this balance (Villalta, 1989).

2 The *Albufera de Valencía* is one of the most important coastal lagoons along the Mediterranean coast. Its natural area is estimated at about thirty thousand hectares, including fluvial marshes. After the drainage of extensive areas for rice cultivation, the surface of the Albufera (which covered 14 000 ha in the eighteenth century), was reduced to 5000 ha in the last part of the nineteenth century; and to just 3000 ha today. As in the Ebro Delta case, the Albufera sustained a well-balanced system of natural resource exploitation, which constituted a local traditional way of life. Various impacts have appeared during the last few decades imperilling its survival, for example water pollution; loss of rice fields because of the introduction of new industrial crops; and urban development projects (Dafauce, 1975; Piera, 1988).

3 The *Aiguamolls de L'Empordà* area originally encompassed approximately thirty-five thousand hectares of fluvial marshes and coastal lagoons. Rice cultivation, begun in the eighteenth century, has reduced this area to only 5000 ha today, or just 14 per cent of the original extent.

Many other wetlands on the Levante coastline, especially "ullales" (coastal lagoons), deltas and fresh marshes (marjalas) have been partially drained for crop production or mosquito control reasons. Accordingly, a large part of the country's original wetland endowment has disappeared. Examples include the Albufera de Elche; the Llobregat Delta; the Prat de Cabanes-Torreblanca; the lagoons of Cullera; the Marjal de Oliva-Pego; and the Marjal de Xeresa. Some others have been completely drained, and nothing is left, for example Peñíscola; Canet; Oriol; Denia; and others (Box, 1987; Pardo, 1987).

On the Atlantic coast, drainage has affected the Cádiz Bay saltmarshes and the Guadalquivir marshes, which have experienced losses of approximately 36 per cent and 62 per cent respectively.

4 The *Laguna de La Janda* was once the largest shallow steppe lake in the Iberian peninsula, with an approximate surface area of four thousand hectares. Reasonably good crop

and cattle production were obtained after this area was drained in the late 1950s. Because of its size and geographical situation, it was originally an internationally important resting point and breeding and wintering area for waterfowl, especially geese. The last known breeding site for crane in Spain was in this wetland (Bernis, 1988).

5 Beginning in the eighteenth century, drainage works were undertaken at *Laguna de La Nava* until finally the last 2000 ha of the original 4000 were converted to irrigated fields in 1950. Economic production on the land has never been very lucrative (Moreno, 1988). Supporting the annual crane migration had been a key role for this wetland, prior to its drainage.

6 A tectonic shallow lake of about three thousand eight hundred hectares at *Laguna de Antela* was an internationally-important waterfowl habitat before it was drained for cultivation in the late 1950s. Antela was the last breeding area of geese in Spain, and the only site frequented by wild swans in the Iberian peninsula. Agricultural production has not been very rewarding.

7 The *Lagunas de La Lantejuela* area is an important endorheic nucleus with nine steppe and shallow saline lakes with a total surface area of about nine hundred hectares. The largest of the shallow lakes were those of Ruiz Sánchez (356 ha) and Calderona (250 ha). Although they had been included in a 1965 list of wetlands of international importance for waterfowl habitat (the MAR list), they were drained for crop production in 1968. The agricultural benefits realized by this process have been mixed. Currently, only two of the shallow lakes with saline waters remain – Ballestera (30 ha) and Calderona Chica (7 ha) (Fajardo and Mazuelos, 1984).

8 The *Llanos de Albacete* area was one of the most important floodplains areas of La Mancha region (12 000 ha). Drainage began in the eighteenth century and continued until the nineteenth century. Crop production and mosquito control were the primary objectives of the drainage activities (López Bermúdez, 1978).

## Dredging

This type of intervention has taken place in many segments of the Guadiana, Ebro, Douro and Segura rivers, primarily for flood prevention and mosquito control. As a result, many floodplains have become permanently dry, and have been cultivated. The most relevant example is that of La Mancha floodplain. Floodplains (25 000 ha) and shallow saline lakes (5000 ha) were the most frequent wetland types. Today, only 10 per cent (5000 ha) of the original floodplain area still remains. These floodplains, together with the associated shallow lakes, were one of the most important areas in Europe for the resting, wintering, and breeding of waterfowl. The region was also included in the MAR list, and in the ICBP and IWRB list of important bird areas in Europe. UNESCO has declared it a Reserve of the Biosphere.

## *Industrial and tourism development*

A significant portion of Spanish coastal wetlands has been affected by large tourism and industrial facilities. Examples include the Mediterranean tourism complexes, and the industrial centre at the Odiel River marshes on the Atlantic coast.

## *Filling*

Cultivation on the land portions of many wetlands has resulted in significant sedimentation or filling of most of Spain's steppe and saline shallow lakes, as well as of some coastal wetlands, such as the Albufera de Valencía or the Guadalquivir marshes.

Many wetland basins are also used as waste reception sites. When the filling process is complete, urbanization then tends to take place, especially at coastal locations.

Several high mountain wetlands and lakes in mountain ranges – Cantabric, Pyrenees, Sierra Nevada – have been affected by ski installations in their watersheds, resulting in increased erosion, sedimentation, and nutrient inputs.

## *Mining of wetland substrata*

Mining for horticultural uses has been the most serious impact suffered by Spanish peatlands. The peatlands of Las Madres and Torreblanca have been seriously damaged in this way. Sand and gravel extraction for the building industry is also a problem in certain riverine and dune wetlands, for example the Corrubedo ponds.

## *Intensive aquaculture*

The main ecological problems here include the physical transformation of the basin; modifications to the hydrological regime; increased nutrient inputs; and the introduction of exotic species. Several aquaculture projects have already had negative impacts in the marshes of Piedras River and Cádiz Bay.

## *Water extraction*

Most Spanish wetlands with fresh or subsaline waters located in arid or semi-arid areas are used, in the dry season, for water supply to support irrigation or industrial needs. This often results in a serious decrease in water levels, which is sometimes lethal for the development of young waterfowl, and for many flora and fauna species. Examples include the Laguna del Taray, and the Carucedo Lake.

Recent research has underlined the importance of groundwater in the hydrological regime of most Spanish wetlands, both coastal and continental. Increasing use of irrigation has depressed the upper limit of many saturated zones in recent years, resulting in the disappearance of, or serious alterations to, several inland wetlands. Important examples of wetlands which have disappeared because of groundwater extraction can be found at Daimiel National Park, Laguna de las Salinas, and Laguna de la Celadilla.

Water extraction can be considered largely as a market failure, resulting from both the absence of effective property rights for water resources; and from the failure of the state to enforce those property rights which do exist.

## *Maintenance of constant water levels*

The basins of temporary water bodies located in arid or semi-arid regions, originally rich in endemic or rare invertebrate and macrophyte species, are often impounded as reservoirs for irrigation, livestock, or fish-production requirements. The biological communities created are usually of less ecological interest. Examples of this problem are found in the Cantalejo ponds, and the Laguna de Sariñena.

## Road construction

Road construction can have a major effect on the hydrologic conditions of some wetlands, especially in fluvio-marine marshes with high tides, for example along the Atlantic coastline. Examples include the new roads crossing the Santoña marshes or Odiel River marshes. This is a clear case of institutional failure, associated with inappropriate land use policy.

## Hydroelectric power production

Many high mountain lakes are interconnected by small-scale systems for hydroelectric power production. These natural hydrological regimes can be greatly disrupted because of sudden and significant variations in water levels (Campas and Villaseca, 1979).

## Alterations in water quality

Waste discharges are adversely affecting the water quality of many Spanish wetlands. Some coastal marshes (for example those of the Odiel River) receive important domestic and industrial sewage inputs. The Albufera de Valencía receives sewage from a human population of 300 000 (36 000 kg/year) and more than 5000 industrial units. The Albufera is currently the most hypereutrophic coastal lagoon in Europe, due to the combination of nutrient loading and agricultural run-off.

Herbicides, pesticides and other agricultural pollutants are another common feature of most catchment areas under cultivation.

Water quality disruption is caused mainly by market failures associated with pollution externalities. The source of these externalities can be either off-site or on-site.

## Introduction of exotic species

The introduction of the Louisiana red swamp crayfish to the Guadalquivir marshes is causing important damage to the functioning of many Spanish wetlands because of the disappearance of prairies of submerged macrophytes. Crayfish overpopulation is particularly threatening to natural resource stability in Doñana National Park.

### *Poaching and uncontrolled seafood exploitation*

Coastal and inland wetlands that lack sufficient warden services often experience conservation problems because of the occasional overexploitation of rare species populations.

### *Changes in littoral plant communities*

The frequent cutting or burning of hydrophyte littoral belts to facilitate access for fishing, hunting or livestock-raising activities, has a negative impact, especially for the breeding of waterfowl.

## Spanish wetland policy in action

### *Agricultural expansion and water depletion*

Spanish arable land accounts for 20.4 million ha (about 40 per cent of the total land area of the country and about 27 per cent of the total arable land within the EC). This area has remained almost unchanged during the past 50 years, suggesting that the conversion of agricultural land to non-agricultural uses has been offset by the incorporation of new land into agricultural use. Since the land area devoted to agriculture has not expanded, the historic increase in agricultural output has resulted almost completely from the intensification of that activity.

A significant contribution to that intensification has come from the expansion of irrigation. In 1920, only 1.35 million ha were supported by irrigation. This figure increased to more than 3.3 million ha in 1986. Between 1977 and 1986 alone, the amount of irrigated land increased by about 13 per cent, while dryland and grassland decreased by 3 and 5 per cent respectively. Significantly for wetlands, about 10 per cent of this growth was based on the increased use of groundwaters.

Associated with these trends has been the intensification of agricultural techniques, the wider use of industrial inputs, and the increasing importance of certain crops. For example, (water-intensive) rice production increased by 16 per cent during the decade 1977–86. Vegetables and fruits have also experienced important volume increases in recent years.

Both the intensification of agriculture and the new crop patterns on some land could only have been achieved by increased use of water. This is a serious problem for a country with a dry climate and an uneven distribution of its water resources. Growing demands for water can be met by increasing the efficiency of irrigation schemes; by damming rivers; or by mining groundwater. Each of these policies ultimately leads to the conversion of wetlands.

At a national scale, Spain has access to more water *per capita* than the European average. The problem is that these resources are very unevenly distributed. More than two-thirds of Spain's water resources are concentrated in about ten per cent of the national area. The capacity of existing dams is 42 000 $hm^3$ (almost ten times that which existed in 1940). This capacity will be increased to 70 000 $hm^3$ as projects already under development come on-line.

Agriculture represents between 85 and 90 per cent of total Spanish water consumption (Llamas, 1988b). Groundwater sources provide almost 30 per cent of these requirements. Between 1962 and 1983, the land area irrigated with groundwater increased from 431 000 ha to about 812 000 ha in 1983 (Garrido, 1989). The fact that only about 100 000 ha of these conversions resulted from state intervention illustrates the important role that the private sector has traditionally played in exploiting groundwater resources.

Private exploitation of groundwater is stimulated by the fact that the required investment is usually relatively small. Productivity per hectare can also be increased quickly, particularly for certain types of agricultural crops – vegetables, fruits, flowers – for which high market prices lead to attractive profits for the farmer. However, it is becoming increasingly clear that the intensive exploitation of groundwater is associated with important external diseconomies. Often, these diseconomies show up in wetland systems.

When groundwater is exploited at less than its rate of replenishment, its consumption by one farmer does not reduce its availability to others. In these circumstances, the lack of effective property rights over the water is not a problem. However, when too many farmers are exploiting the "public" aquifer, the absence of defined rights of ownership immediately becomes a problem. This is the situation that is presently occurring in many areas of Spain.

Groundwater is more important in some regions than in other. For example, in Castilla-La Mancha, groundwater provides more than 60 per cent of the irrigated water requirement while in Aragon or Extremadura, the groundwater contributes only 3 and 5 per cent, respectively. The Castilla-La Mancha figure is particularly important for this study, since this region contains one of the most important wetland areas in Spain: The Tablas de Daimiel National Park.

## *Tablas de Daimiel*

The Tablas de Daimiel is located in the natural semi-arid region of La Mancha (Central Plateau). It includes a floodplain of about 8600 ha near the confluence of two relatively small rivers, the Gigüela and the Guadiana (total basin size of about 15 000 $km^2$). It constitutes the natural discharge zone of a Tertiary aquifer system, which is about 100 m thick, and which extends over an area of some 5000 $km^2$. This is one of the most important and best-known aquifers of the Iberian peninsula. It is also an internationally-important wetland.

The park was created in 1973. The objective of the Protection Act of 1980 was mainly to preserve the water control regulation functions within the park's wetlands. However, it must be noted that the National Park itself includes only about 2000 ha while the complete wetland area is about 8600 ha. Therefore, the protection provided by the creation of the park alone will obviously be insufficient for conserving the total wetland. Furthermore, because the wetland is itself an integral part of a larger system, the Guadiana river basin, any changes that occur upstream of the basin, are likely to affect not only the total wetland, but also the Damiel area.

Only 25 years ago, La Mancha region was one of the most extensive dryland farming regions in Spain. At that time, an important underground aquifer was discovered. Irrigated land expanded from 30 000 ha in 1974 to more than 125 000 ha in 1987. Consequently, irrigation requirements increased dramatically between 1974 and 1987, accelerating the depletion of the very aquifer so fundamental to the health of the Tablas de

Daimiel. Pumpage from the aquifer increased from 200 $hm^3$ in 1974 to 600 $hm^3$ in 1987. As a result, there has been a progressive and generalized depletion of the water table (Llamas, 1988a). Tablas de Daimiel ceased to be a discharge area for the aquifer in 1984. By 1986, there was almost no water left in the Tablas, even during the wet season.

Among the other anthropogenic interventions that have affected the Tablas de Daimiel park, the desiccation laws enacted between 1960 and 1970, concerning the shallow water areas of the Gigüela, Zácara, Riansares and Guadiana rivers, are noteworthy. The objective of these Acts was to develop nearly 30 000 ha for agriculture. A second indirect intervention has been the dredging of the Guadiana, and the opening of drainage channels. Both of these interventions resulted in the reduction of local water levels.

Expansion of agricultural activity, together with reductions in water levels ultimately led to increased soil salinization. The water of the Gigüela River is naturally rich in salts. This natural problem was exacerbated by the typically poor design and low operating efficiency of the new irrigation systems. The result was a reduced capacity of the water system to cleanse itself of salts.

Water quality in the region is also deteriorating because of the increased use of chemical inputs like fertilizers and pesticides. (From 1955 to 1985, the consumption of nitrogen compounds in Spain increased from 2880 to 99 630 tonnes, while phosphate use increased from 12 060 to 61 856, and potassium expanded from 4680 to 33 921 tonnes.)

Despite the creation of the National Park, and the implementation of other national and international protection measures such as the Integral Reserve of Scientific Interest, the Ramsar list and the Biosphere Reserve, the hydrologic regime of the Tablas de Damiel has been drastically changed. The deterioration implicit in these changes had been denounced for several years in scientific papers, all of which had been disregarded by the authorities (López Camacho, 1987). The most important reasons for this disregard included:

(i) the traditional attitude of hydraulic engineers within the Guadiana Water Authority, who ignored the ecological importance of groundwater; and

(ii) the economic and social development that exploitation of the groundwaters was supporting in the region (Llamas, 1988a).

La Mancha aquifer was declared overexploited under the new Spanish Water Act, and several technical measures were planned for the so-called Restoration Plan for the Tablas de Daimiel. However, the Act stated that existing farming interests were not to be affected by this plan. In effect, no potential reorganization of the irrigated area, based on available water resources, was to be undertaken. Instead, a very expensive (more than US$8million) solution was proposed. This solution required the importing of water, 60 $hm^3$ over a three year period, from another watershed to replenish the Tablas. Not surprisingly, this measure has been unsuccessful in restoring the original ecological processes of the Tablas de Damiel mainly because it was unable to restore the natural fluctuations and dynamics of that wetland system. The only effective ecological solution would be to reduce pumping activities – an approach with obvious political ramifications. Some experts think that the degree of deterioration has now advanced to such a point that restoration would be almost impossible, given the economic and social costs involved.

This case provides a typical example of the conflict between short-term economic interests and long-term environmental consequences. The immediate monetary benefits are easy to identify and calculate, while the long-term deterioration of the ecosystem, and, importantly, the economic implications of such deterioration, are harder to perceive and to express in monetary terms.

In effect, the benefits of agricultural development in areas adjacent to the Tablas de Daimiel have been overvalued from a social point of view because they fail to take into account the present and future social and ecological costs of that exploitation on the Tablas de Daimiel, or of the surrounding wetland ecosystem, of which it is an integral part. These benefits are also overvalued because they fail to consider the loss of (non-marketable) social and ecological benefits that would be realized if the wetland were not altered.

In the Tablas de Daimiel, Spain faces a case of depletion externalities, resulting from the fact that there are no legal or institutional mechanisms to regulate use, either through the assignment of property rights, or through regulations that prevent individuals from over-appropriating the resource. The Tablas de Damiel situation is, in fact, even more complex than this, since the overexploitation of water results not only in the reduced supplies for other farmers, but also in the disruption of the environmental and economic role of a nearby natural ecosystem.

## *The Bajo Guadalquivir case*

The Guadalquivir marsh area is the most important wetland in Spain. However, in this case, the scale and the complexity of the wetland management problem are significantly larger than in the Tablas de Damiel. While the Tablas de Daimiel is a protected area of 1928 ha, the Coto de Doñana is a protected area of 50 720 ha in a natural region known as Marismas del Guadalquivir, located at the mouth of one of the largest fluvial watersheds in the Iberian peninsula.

The Marismas del Guadalquivir is an extensive geomorphological unit of 3000 km². Prior to its transformation earlier this century, it was a territory of little production, and it was largely uninhabited.

The saltmarsh portion of the basin has been under intense agricultural pressure since 1930. Presently, only 52 000 ha of the marsh have been preserved in a more or less natural state, while 82 000 (62 per cent) are being cultivated (Ojeda, 1987). All the transformed marsh is located on the left bank. (The creation of the Doñana National Park prevented the conversion of the right bank.) Those areas with the most abundant freshwater influence – Isla Mayor, Isla Minima – were the first to be converted, principally for rice production. About forty per cent of Spanish rice production occurs here. The rest of the left bank was intensively transformed during the 1960s reaching a total area of 67 270 ha of irrigated fields – with maize, sunflower and cotton being the primary crops on this land.

Although the left bank marshes had been transformed without any apparent conflict, plans to convert the right bank faced great protests because of growing national and international awareness of the ecological value of the area. The first Doñana

National Park boundaries were established in 1969.

Historically, agriculture has been the backbone of the Andalusian economy. Regional climatic conditions permit the culture of certain crops during long periods of the year. Outputs supply the European market, where they (presently) attract relatively high prices. As explained earlier, these cultures create severe impacts on the environment, because of their high demand for water, and their intensive use of chemical inputs.

A study of the agricultural potential of the area was initiated during the 1960s by FAO and IGME (Instituto Geológico y Minero). The existence of a large aquifer motivated planning for an irrigation project intended to be the most important groundwater-based irrigation project in Spain (24 000 ha) – the Almonte-Marismas Irrigation Plan. Subsequently, the assumptions underlying this analysis were found to be too optimistic, and the proposal was reduced to 15 000 ha. The first areas developed were those next to sandy soils, for which the level of public support amounted to about US$132 million (Llamas, 1988a). By 1986, 7000 hectares of irrigated fields had been developed by 1986, at a yearly pumping rate of some 50 $hm^3$. At present about 10 000 ha have been transformed – 3000 more than recommended by IGME as a threshold necessary to avoid ecological damages. And there are still new irrigation projects being planned. In addition to the significant loadings of fertilizers and pesticides that enter the park through surface run-off, there is also nitrate pollution occurring in the groundwaters that discharge in the park.

The Marismas del Guadalquivir has also been greatly affected by the mass tourism that developed in Spain during the last few decades. An important related development has been the growth of El Rocío – until the 1950s, a small village which functions as the "gate" to the Guadalquivir wetland. El Rocío is located at the point of convergence of several different ecosystems. Historically El Rocío has been the site of one of Spain's most important religious pilgrimages. In 1981, the "Fiesta del Rocío" attracted one million people.

Another important tourism development occurred in the coastal area of Huelva. Tourism development plans for the Huelva coast called for the number of residential units to expand from 33 000 to 341 200 between 1964 and 1984, that is more than 10 times in less than 20 years. Adjacent to the park, the small fishing village of Matalascañas has also become an important tourism centre, receiving as many as 100 000 people during the summer season. Drinking water supplies are derived from aquifers. There are new tourism projects now being planned, which would further increase demands. The accumulated impacts of all these projects could cause saltwater intrusion and the eventual salinization of the nearby pits and dune ponds.

It is worth noting that from Torre Higuera to the outfall of the Guadalquivir, the coast is partially privately owned. Moreover, about thirty-six per cent of the total area of the Doñana National Park itself is privately owned. Conversely, the government has been the promoter and principal agent of virtually all agricultural and tourism development in the region. (Recall that, in the case of Tablas de Daimiel, the expansion of irrigation resulted largely from *private* initiatives.)

Although still there are as yet no clearly visible symptoms of the real depletion that is probably occurring in the piezometric levels in the Park, there are several hydrogeological models that predict decreases of between one and ten metres in the groundwater levels. Serious ecological consequences, including the disappearing of wetlands in the dunes and ecotone would result from such a decline. The problem is that when these effects eventually materialize, it will by then be very difficult to find effective political and economic solutions. Unfortunately, in the case of Doñana, there is simply not enough knowledge about the hydrologic functioning of the area to make reliable projections (Hollis et al., 1988).

Stresses caused by agricultural, tourism, and residential development are the major sources of the environmental impacts in the Marismas. However, there are other problems, including mining activity at Aznalcollar; and plantation forestry (eucalyptus), which is increasingly replacing the natural forests, and which is known for its high demands for water. Clearly, environmental assessments in the region must weigh the cumulative impacts of all forms of development interventions.

Social and institutional conflict concerning land use – agriculture, tourism and environmental protection – had to arise given these competing interests. This conflict is also played out within government agencies. For example, the Institute for Agricultural Development and Reform (IARA) of

Andalusia promotes irrigation, while a division of the Ministry of Agriculture, the Institute for Nature Conservation (ICONA) is responsible for managing the National Park – but in such a way as to protect the environment without compromising agricultural development. Various forms of legal instruments exist, declaring the area a National Touristic Interest Site (1969); a National Interest Area for Irrigation Transformation (1971); and a National Park (1969). This contradictory policy reflects the total lack of a coherent land-use policy, based on the government's attempts to satisfy many different social interests simultaneously (Cruz, 1988).

It bears repeating that the existence of the park in itself does not guarantee the survival of the wetland. Not only is the park just a small fraction of the complete wetland, but the borders of the park are not even well-defined. Nor do they coincide with any particular ecosystem, so important parts of the wetland remain outside the park, and largely under private ownership.

## *Monegros*

The endorheic nucleus, known as Monegros Sur, is one of the most rare wetland complexes in both the Iberian peninsula and, indeed, in western Europe. The system contains more than 90 shallow steppe wetlands, including 15 shallow saline lakes, of great environmental variability. Numerous rare species of flora and fauna live here. Valuable geomorphological and sedimentological processes also occur in the area. The human population has traditionally been well-adapted to the arid conditions of the area. Historically, the Monegros region has been among the least developed in Spain. As a result, the new Irrigation Project (Monegros II) seeks to increase the economic potential of the region by extracting water from several tributaries of the Ebro River.

The cost of Monegros II is projected to be about US$727 million over a period of 20 years. The project will convert 66 000 ha into an irrigated area for plant and animal agriculture. Increases in both agricultural production, and employment are anticipated with the project.

However, some authors indicate that about 67 per cent of the area to be converted will suffer an acceleration of soil salinization, which would eventually result in *reductions* in expected crop production; and in increased salinization of groundwater supplies.

It is likely that conversion will also produce several undesirable effects, such as the loss of important species of scientific interest, and modification of the wetland from a seasonally inundated system to a permanently inundated one (Pedrocchi et al., 1988).

Furthermore, if additional drainage systems are installed to combat the risk of salinization in the converted areas, the most likely consequence will be an even larger discharge of salts into the Ebro, with the unavoidable result that agricultural land in downstream reaches of the Ebro will be damaged.

The anticipated indirect consequences of the Monegros II project have scarcely been considered in planning the project. They are not visible to, nor do they specifically harm the interests of, the population in the area to be converted. On the other hand, they are poorly understood by the people living in downstream areas.

The Monegros case illustrates several important problems in the management of Spanish wetlands:

(i) environmental effects caused upstream, affecting third parties downstream (i.e. externalities);
(ii) difficulties in valuing both irreversible damage and unique environments; and
(iii) environmental values tend to be relatively "income elastic", and these values will probably be highest at the very moment when "good quality" water from the Ebro will be in short supply.

## *The Mar Menor case*

Coastal wetlands and coastal lagoons provide different services from those discussed in the earlier cases. Besides, their conversion is typically motivated by other interests, and the type of intervention is also different. The conflicts and methodological difficulties inherent in the coastal situation are illustrated by the case of the Mar Menor, one of the most important coastal lagoons on the Spanish Mediterranean coast.

The conversion of the Mar Menor area has been occurring

for a long time. However, the reasons for its conversion have changed. Originally, conversion responded to agricultural or fishery development pressures. Today, the driving force is tourism.

Especially along the Mediterranean coast, a major cause of wetland loss is drainage or filling for urban or industrial development. Compared to the surface area lost due to agricultural expansion, the geographic impact of this type of intervention seems rather small. However, the environmental significance is much larger.

As in other countries, the rate of loss of coastal wetlands is closely correlated with increases in population densities. An important population migration process has taken place in Spain during the last decade. With rapid economic growth there has been an acceleration in the urbanization of coastal areas. Urbanization and population pressure are often imposed on essentially fragile wetland ecosystems. This is what is happening in the Mar Menor Lagoon.

## Summary and conclusions

Because of their open and transitional character, as well as their geographical locations, Spanish wetlands are very complex systems. They are of great value in both the national and international context. They offer a wide range of potential services and functions that can be used by many different social groups.

Spanish shallow-water environments are "crossing points" where many different interests converge, making it difficult to develop rational policies for their management. This problem is aggravated by a lack of knowledge about how they function. A comprehensive inventory, financed by the Spanish government, is now being completed, so information about the actual magnitude of the national wetland endowment, and ongoing trends in that endowment, should be available soon.

Spain has lost an estimated 60 per cent of its original wetland area. This loss can be linked to the fundamental economic and demographic transformations that have occurred within Spanish society, especially during the last three decades.

Even though government interest in wetland issues has

increased noticeably in recent years, motivated partly by Spain joining the EC and partly by the signing of several international agreements on the environment, the process of wetland destruction has not completely stopped. One thing that has changed, however, is that indirect interventions are becoming much more important, relative to direct ones, than was the case in the past.

Several laws have recently been enacted dealing directly with wetland conservation. This has created a useful legal framework for future protection. In this regard, the declaration that all inland waters, both surficial and ground, belong to the public is an important step forward.

Agriculture is still the main cause of degradation of inland wetlands. However, the emphasis in this pressure has shifted from land reclamation to increased demands for water supplies, for example irrigation. Spanish membership in the EC has aggravated agricultural pressure on wetlands because Community agricultural policy is based on productivity criteria without regard to the environmental endowments of individual countries. This lack of flexibility in EC policy is having a great impact on Spanish agro-systems due to three complementary processes – intensification, speicalization, and changes in land uses. The result is that short-term benefits are pursued and surplus production occurs. In turn, this leads to the overexploitation of natural resources; to chemical pollution by fertilizers and pesticides; and to the destruction of natural habitats.

In this context, Spanish agricultural policy has actively promoted irrigation projects, despite the semi-arid nature of the country. Not surprisingly, excess water demands have led to the irrational overexploitation of some aquifers. The development of irrigation projects based on groundwaters is causing serious conservation problems in important Spanish wetlands. This overexploitation is seriously altering the hydrologic regimes in these areas, sometimes causing their complete desiccation. Overexploitation can also reduce future irrigation possibilities, threatening the continuity of the very crop production they were established to assist, for example, in the La Mancha wetlands. Even irrigation using surfice water has deleterious effects on wetlands. Lowlands (where wetlands normally occur) are usually irrigated first because water transport is cheapest there.

**Table 5.1: Major causes of Spanish wetland loss and degradation**

| | MARKET FAILURES EXTERNALITIES | | | | |
|---|---|---|---|---|---|
| **WETLAND** | **Pollution externalities** | | | | **Property** |
| **TYPES** | **Air pollution off-site** | **Water pollution off-site** | **Water pollution on-site** | **Congestion costs on-site** | **rights externalities** |
| *Mountain wetlands and lakes* | | eutrophication, waste discharge | recreation pressure, waste discharge | cattle pressure | |
| *Steppe and saline shallow lakes* | | discharge of trash<br>domestic sewage and agricultural run-off | | | overexploitation of groundwater |
| *Dune field wetlands* | | pollution due to agricultural activities | pollution due to agricultural development | | overexploitation of groundwater |
| *Floodplains* | | pollution by agriculture | pollution by agriculture<br>sewage from human settlements | | overexploitation of groundwater |
| *Peatlands* | | | | | |
| *Coastal wetlands* | industrial urban pollution | industrial pollution and urban pollution | | | |

INTERVENTION FAILURES

| Intersectoral policy inconsistency | | | Counterproducts wetland policy |
|---|---|---|---|
| **Competing sector output prices** | **Competing sector output prices** | **Land-use policy** | **Institutional failures** |
| hydroelectric exploitation: fluctuation of water levels | | ski installations (tourism) | |
| drainage for crop production | hunting pressure | waste disposal | drainage for mosquito control<br><br>Lousiana red crayfish<br><br>filling by alteration of watershed |
| sand mining for construction | | | |
| drainage for crop production | | direct conversion for health programme<br><br>channels for flood protection<br><br>agricultural conversion<br><br>peat mining for agricultural uses | |
| seafood exploitation pressure<br><br>hunting | | land reclamation for tourism and industrial development<br><br>intensive aquaculture<br><br>road construction | Lousiana red crayfish |

Agricultural transformation, pollution problems and changes in the flooding regime then follow.

Tourism and urban demands for land are main factors threatening the future of coastal wetlands. The high percentage (40 per cent) of occupied land along Spanish coasts makes it difficult to conserve any remaining wetlands that become isolated.

The degradation of Spanish wetlands continues because, despite of the existence of a legal structure for their protection, there is no effective administrative and institutional apparatus for their management. The administrative network related to wetlands management is so complex that it is difficult to design effective management policies. It is clear that national wetland policy should be the responsibility of a single agency. Such a policy should be developed and implemented in co-ordination with the Autonomous Regions. The Ramsar-España Committee might be the appropriate body to undertake this function, and to apply the same directives to the Spanish administrative structure that the central bureau of Ramsar applies to the international co-ordination of wetlands.

In the long run, only *preventive* measures can be successful in conserving wetland systems. It is obvious from past experience that projects which have already been started are very difficult to stop. In addition, projects for ecologic restoration also have little chance of success, due to the lack of knowledge of how wetlands actually function.

In general, existing economic evaluation methodologies tend to over-value present (marketable) private benefits, and under-value long-term (unmarketable) social costs. Even the identification of wetland services is often insufficient to support a proper valuation of wetlands (leaving aside the problem of quantification). Three "qualitative" dimensions of wetlands deserve special attention in the Spanish context. These are the size and diversity of the wetland complex; the interrelationship between the wetland and its surrounding areas; and the nature of adjacent ecosystems.

It is typical for the delineation of the wetland to be based on administrative criteria, rather than ecological ones. It can be controversial to consider some areas as "wetland units" in themselves, since they are really part of larger ecosystems. For this reason, contiguous ecosystems should be examined in relation to the type, frequency, duration and magnitude of the interaction. These factors are likely to have an important role in the valuation of functions such as water quality enhancement, flood control, and wildlife preservation.

The most important market and intervention failures in Spanish wetland management are related to the following problems:

- wetlands are usually common property (i.e. public goods);
- public intervention on wetlands is likely to change the opportunities for realizing environmental goods and services, and therefore the distribution of these outputs;
- intervention activities are not necessarily undertaken in the wetland itself. Similarly, interventions on wetlands are likely to affect surrounding systems;
- interventions have long-run, cumulative effects that are difficult to anticipate and to quantify;
- intervention will often produce irreversible effects (depletion of resources, definitive conversion of wetlands); and
- policy measures concerning interventions on wetlands will always face some uncertainty.

The major types of market and intervention failures in Spanish wetlands are structured and summarized in table 5.1.

A national policy for the wise use of Spanish wetlands should include at least the following elements:

1 Creation of a government agency for the co-ordination, control and harmonization of the different policies of autonomic and central administrative bodies.
2 Improvements to the Environmental Impact Assessment process, so these studies would have to include any activities likely to affect wetland conservation variables. (It is particularly important that irrigation and rural development projects include an EIA in their design.)
3 The creation of tax and economic incentives for private landowners and industries to promote the conservation and wise use of wetlands. An existing law on Systems for Promoting the Improvement of the Agricultural Structures (1987) provides an institutional framework for this kind of measure.

4 Incorporation in EC agricultural policy of the "multiple function" principle, so the sustainable use of natural resources receives as much priority as increases in agricultural output.
5 A basic problem facing the rational management of Spanish wetlands is that many of them are privately owned. Because wetland services cannot be easily valued in monetary terms, and because of the "public good" character of wetlands, private owners have little incentive to preserve resources which are, from their point of view, virtually free. One solution may be to transfer the most important wetlands to public ownership.
6 Increased financial support for the management of already-protected wetlands. Since most of these have only recently been created, it is necessary to develop an overall structure for the achievement of stated protection goals.
7 Increased financial support for research activities on the structure and functioning of Spanish wetlands.
8 Land management programmes should regard wetlands as integral units of Spanish territory, as well as recognize their socio-economic importance. However, boundaries of protected sites should be established in accordance with *natural*, rather than *political*, limits.
9 Criteria for selecting new wetlands to be protected should take into account not only rare species or unique sites, but should also include special relationships or processes that may exist within the wetland and between the wetland and other systems. A policy of protecting isolated wetlands is insufficient.
10 A "precautionary" policy of retaining adequate representation of key ecological features is an important step, given the present lack of scientific understanding that exists about these processes.
11 A holistic approach should be adopted for the management of wetlands. For example, the present approach, which favours biotic over abiotic aspects, should be avoided.
12 A complete and open inventory of wetlands, including ecological types is necessary.
13 Training of wetland management experts must be increased. It is particularly necessary to spread hydrogeological and ecological knowledge at all administrative

levels (decision-makers, government officials and users).
14 Education and awareness-promotion programmes concerning nature for children and adults must be undertaken.
15 Increasing economic pressure on wetlands illustrates that the public is aware of its significant economic value. Unfortunately, market prices do not fully reflect all values of wetlands. This suggests that better economic assessments of wetland resources should be routinely performed. In particular, economic criteria for using wetlands should be established and used.

## References

Alonso, M., *Las Lagunas de la España Peninsular: Taxonomía, Ecología y Distribucíon de los Cládoceros*. Tesis Doctoral (Universidad de Barcelona, 1985).

Alonso, M., "Clasificación de los Complejos Palustres Españoles", *Bases Científicas para la Protección de los Humedales en España*, Real Academia de Ciencias de Madrid, pp.65–78 (1987).

Alonso, M. and M. Comelles, "Criterios Básicos para la Clasificación Limnológica de las Masas de Agua Continentales de Pequeño Volumen de España", *Actas del Primer Congreso de Limnología*, pp.35–49 (1981).

Alonso, M. and M. Comelles, "A Preliminary Grouping of the Small Epicontinental Water Bodies in Spain and Distribution of Crustacea and Charophyta", *Verh. Internat. Verein. Limnol.*, vol. 22, pp.1699–703 (1984).

Bernaldez, F. G. and C. Montes (co-ord.), *Inventario y Tipología Basada en su Génesis y Funcionamiento de los Humedales del Acuífero de Madrid Canal de Isabel II* (Comunidad de Madrid, 1989).

Bernis, F., "El Ocaso de los Humedales Españoles", *Quercus*, vol. 34, pp.22–6 (1988).

Box, M., *Humedales y Áreas Lacustres de la Provincia de Alicante* Instituto de Estudios Juan Gil Albert (1987).

Campas, L. L. and J. M. Villaseca, "Els Llacs Pirinencs", *Quad. Ecol. Apl.*, vol. 4, pp.25–36 (1979).

Cowardin, L. M., V. Carter, F. C. Golet and E. T. LaRoe, *Classification of Wetlands and Deepwater Habitats of the United States* (Washington DC: US Fish & Wildlife Service Pub. FWS/OBS-79/31, 1979).

Cruz, J., "La Intervención del Hombre en la Ría y Marismas del Guadalquivir", *Eria*, pp.109–23 (1988).

Dafauce, C., *La Albufera de Valencia: un Estudio Piloto* (Madrid:

ICONA. Monografía 4, 1975).

Diaz del Olmo, F. and F. Molina, "Parques Naturales Andaluces: una Estrategia de Conservación y Desarrollo en Regiones Deprimidas", *Revista de Estudios Andaluces*, vol. 4, pp.147–56 (1985).

DGMA, *Medio ambiente en España* (Madrid: MOPU, 1986).

Fajardo, A. and M. Mazuelos, "El Área Endorreica de la Lantejuerela: Requiem por una Zona Húmeda de Importancia Internacional", *Quercus*, vol. 12, pp.34–6 (1984).

Fernández-Cruz, M. (co-ord.), *Clasificación de las Zonas Húmedas Españolas en Función de las Aves Acuáticas* (Madrid: Sociedad Española de Ornitología, 1987).

Fernández-Cruz, M., R. Marti, A. Martinez-Abrain and J. Monreal, "Las Zonas Húmedas Españolas y su Importancia Relativa a la Luz de los Censos de Aves Acuáticas Realizados por la Sociedad Española de Ornitología", *Zonas Húmedas Ibéricas*, pp.61–8 (Valencia: Center Verd., 1988).

Garrido, L., "El Regadıó en España: Importancia de la Agricultura de Regadıó con Aguas Subterráneas", *Jornadas Jurídico-técnicas sobre las Aguas Subterráneas en la Nueva Legislación de Aguas* (Madrid, 1987).

Gonzalez-Perez, J., J. Toledo and C. Arrieta, *Comentarios a la Ley de Aguas. Civitas* (Madrid, 1987).

Hammer, U. T., "Saline Lake Ecosystems of the World" *Junk. Publ.* (1986).

Hollis, T. et al., *The Implications of Groundwater Extraction for the Long Term Future of the Doñana National Park* (Report for WWF, 1989).

Llamas, M. R., "Conflicts between Wetland Conservation and Groundwater Exploitation: Two Case Histories in Spain", *Environ. Geol. Water. Sci.*, vol. 11, no. 3, pp.241–51 (1988a).

Llamas, M. R., "Evolución del Conocimiento y del Aprovechamiento de las Aguas Subterráneas en España", *Jornadas Sobre la Aplicación de la Nueva Ley de Aguas en la Gestión de las Aguas Subterráneas*, Zaragoza, pp.3–32 (1988b).

López-Bermúdez, F., "El Sector Pantanoso al W de Albacete y su Desecación", *Al-Basite*, vol. 5, pp.69–80 (1978).

Lopez-Camacho, B., "Hidrología de las Tablas de Daimiel", *Seminario sobre bases científicas para la protección de los humedales en España* (Madrid, 1987).

Martin-Novella, C. et al., "Zonas Húmedas y Aves Acuáticas", Quercus, vol. 34, pp.16–21 (1988).

Martínez-Parra, P., "Las Zonas Húmedas en la Ley de Aguas", Quercus, vol. 34, pp.43–5 (1988a).

Martínez-Parra, P., "La Protección de las Zonas Húmedas en la

Legislación de Aguas", *II Jornadas Ibéricas sobre Estudio y Protección de las Zonas Húmedas*, pp.35–43 (1988b).
Metra Seis, *Turismo cinegético en España* (Madrid: Secretaría General de Turismo), 221pp. (1985).
Mistch, W. and K. Gosselink, *Wetlands* (New York: Van Nostrand, 1986).
Montes, C. and P. Martino, "Las Lagunas Salinas Españolas", *Bases Científicas para la Protección de los Humedales en España*, pp.95–145. Real Academia de Ciencias de Madrid (1987).
Montes, C. and P. Martin de Agar, "Los Humedales Españoles como Elementos del Paisaje Ibérico", *Arbor*, pp. 518–9: 75–93 (1989).
Montes, C. (ed.), *Zonas Humedas Continentales de España. Inventanio, Tipitiacion, Relacìon Con el Régimen Hidrico General* (Madrid: Direccion General de Obras Hidraulicas, MOPV, Madrid, 1990).
Moreno, I., "Como Borrar del Mapa una Zona Húmeda", *Quercus*, vol. 34, pp.27–8 (1988).
Morillo, C. (ed.), *Lista Roja de los Vertebrados de España* (Madrid: ICONA, 1986).
Ojeda, J. F., *Organización del Territorio en Doñana y su Entorno Próximo (Almonte)*, Siglos XVIII–XX (Madrid: ICONA, 1987).
Pardo, L., *El Aprovechamiento Biológico Integral de las Aguas Dulces* (Madrid: Ministerio de Agricultura, 1942).
Pardo, L., *Catálogo de los Lagos de España*, Inst. Forest. Invest. Exp. Biología de las Aguas Continentales VI. (Ministerio de Agricultura, 1948).
Pardo, R., "Estado Actual de las Zonas Húmedas del Pais Valenciá", *Zonas Húmedas Ibéricas*, pp.79–87 (Valencia: FAT, El Centre Verd., 1987).
Pedrocchi, C., *Evaluación Preliminar del Impacto Ambiental de los Regadıós en el Polígono Monegros II* (Huesca: Instituto Pirenaico de Ecología (CSIC). Jaca, 1988).
Piera, E., *El Cas de L'Albufera: Zones Humides Valencianes* Generalitat Valenciana (1988).
Troya, A., "El Convenio de Ramsar", Quercus, vol. 36, pp.36–40 (1989).
Velez, F., *Impactos sobre Zones Humedas Naturales*. ICONA, Monografia, No. 20 (Madrid: MAPA, 1979).
Villalta, A., "La Importancia del Delta del Ebro", *La Garcilla*, vol. 74, pp.18–24 (1989).

# INDEX